"Life's too short not to be real. I hope kids can see themselves in us. Christians deal with real issues and have real struggles and that's OK." — *Scotla*

Some Kind Of
JOURNEY
ON THE ROAD WITH AUDIO ADRENALINE

Some Kind Of JOURNEY

ON THE ROAD WITH AUDIO ADRENALINE

SEVEN DAYS. SEVEN ISSUES. SEVEN SOULS.

Standard Publishing
Cincinnati, Ohio

Project manager and editor: Dale Reeves
Journalist: Ginny McCabe
Road pastor: Jim Burgen
Cover art direction: Kerri Stuart
Cover and inside design: Dina Sorn
Photography: Chad Angone, Rachel Eichenberger, David Liggitt, Ginny McCabe, Julie Munos, Dale Reeves
Videography: Eric Hannah, Stephanie Fitch, Jeff Lawson
Audio Adrenaline management: True Artist Management
Project coordination and video stills: Scott Brickell, Mark Nicholas
Concert bookings: William Morris Agency
Special thanks to the families of AudioA and the seven souls for childhood photos

"Did You Know?" stats used by permission and taken from the following sources:
Issue 1—Children's Defense Fund; <u>Thirteenth Gen: Abort, Retry, Ignore, Fail?</u>
by William Strauss, et al., Random House, 1993.
Issue 2—<u>Generation Next: What You Need to Know About Today's Youth,</u>
by George Barna, Regal, 1995.
Issue 3—AP News Service, April 11, 1996; Youthviews, February 28, 1997.
Issue 4—American Psychological Association Monitor, September, 1995.
Issue 6—USA Today, June 11, 18, 1997.
Issue 7—Reader's Digest, September 1996; <u>Right from Wrong: What You Need to Know to Help Youth Make the Right Choices</u>, by Josh McDowell and Bob Hostetler, Word Publishing, 1994.

AudioVision CD produced by John Hampton. Executive producers: Dan R. Brock, Eddie DeGarmo. AudioVision CD © The ForeFront Communications Group, Inc., 201 Seaboard Ln., Franklin, TN 37067 (615) 771-2900. International Copyright Secured. All rights reserved. Unauthorized reproduction of this recording is prohibited by Federal Law.

The Standard Publishing Company, Cincinnati, Ohio
A Division of Standex International Corporation

04   03   02   01   00   99   98   97   5   4   3   2   1

CONTENTS

FOREWORD

It has been almost a year since we first dreamed of taking a group of young adults out on tour with us. (This idea initially came from the song, "Free Ride," which is recorded on our BLOOM record.) We wanted to have a diverse group of kids from all over the country travel with us on tour so that we could get to know them and they could have a glimpse into our lives and experience what a tour is really like. As planning started for the week-long trip, we decided to take along a youth pastor to mediate discussions about different topics that need attention within our culture and the church today. A camera crew and journalists were also invited to capture the week. Students from across the country sent in video applications and a group of seven emerged.

The trip was an intense week of late nights, wild and reckless adventure, and meaningful discussions. Friendships were built and guards were let down. Opinions and ideas flew over an array of different topics. By the week's end, we all had a better view of the diversity of the body of Christ and the challenges young people face daily. This is an intense look at what God is doing in this generation.

We are excited about this book and the honest way in which the group wrestled with these topics. It is our prayer that this book will not only entertain, but also bring to light God's truth as it pertains to issues that are uncomfortable and controversial. This book and the trip it documents may be one of the most meaningful things we, as a band, have been privileged to be a part of.

Enjoy and be challenged by SOME KIND OF JOURNEY.
—Audio Adrenaline
September, 1997

PREVIEW

Welcome to SOME KIND OF JOURNEY

Seven Days • Seven Issues • Seven Souls

"The idea to take some people on the road with us started with the song 'Free Ride.' Initially, we wanted to have kids ride along with Audio Adrenaline as a contest, but it developed into a lot more than that," says singer Mark Stuart. The trip with Audio Adrenaline was planned with seven different people, who addressed seven current issues—in seven short days. Each person submitted a video application before the tour. "We wanted this road trip to include a diverse group of people. Many kids out there are dealing with a variety of issues. I think it's going to really hit home with many of them," Mark adds.

Those on the road with AudioA included Chad Angone, age 19, from Littleton, CO; Rachel Eichenberger, age 19, from Cincinnati, OH; Vicki Laine, age 21, from Danville, CA; Scotia Little, age 21, from Bowie, MD; David Liggitt, age 18, from Dallas, TX; Lisa Sampson, age 22, from Huntington Beach, CA; and John Whitton, age 18, from Mission Viejo, CA.

issue #1
Hard to Handle

Seven strangers discuss their lives and the difficult challenges they face. This talk centers around depression, apathy and God's sustaining strength through tough times. In the words of Scotia, "I think people deal with situations the best way they know how in order to survive. Denial is depression and it can damage your emotions when you suppress it. What happens is you let it dwell within you. Then, you find out the only way that's going to be long-lasting is through God."

This talk began at Nashville Speedway U.S.A., but several of the drivers ran trial laps, so we completed the majority of the talk outside at Bongo Java, a coffeehouse near Belmont University. (Often, you'll find artists and songwriters hanging out there. In fact, we spotted Sarah Masen on the porch reading.)

issue #2
Black and White in a Gray World

Whatever happened to right and wrong? Does anything go? Comments about this issue range from Vicki, "You need to be true to yourself, you need to be real" to road pastor Jim Burgen, "What if you're sincerely wrong? Is it wrong for all people, all times, all places?"

"I believe in the Bible 100%. You have to believe in it all the way. I know that Jesus died on the cross for us and God loves us. These are absolute truths. I have this incredible love for God. He rocks!" affirms Chad. In the words of Lisa, "The bottom line is that God calls us to hate sin. Either Jesus is the truth, or he's a liar. There is grace when we slip and fall. We can come to God and say, 'God, I hate this and I don't want to do this. Please help me overcome this.' That's what grace is all about." This conversation takes an honest look at our struggles and his grace.

issue #3
The Church: Hospital or Country Club?

What is the condition of the church today? Is it a place where people go to experience God or a meeting together of the social elite? This talk reveals how the church is viewed by this generation. David Liggitt observes, "Many people are looking for a relationship with God, but they won't necessarily come to church. . . . I think when you witness to them, you get out of your comfort zone." AudioA's drummer, Ben, talks about the fact that some churches seem to prejudge you, based on your appearance. Frontman Mark Stuart adds, "The job of the church is to meet people's needs and introduce them to Christ." It was concluded that God deserves our best 24 hours a day, seven days a week—not just on Sunday.

issue #4
For Better, for Worse . . . or Until I Change My Mind

Will McGinniss talks about his childhood: "I didn't really have a [positive] father figure in my life. When I discovered that God desired to be my Abba Father [intimate Daddy], I really took hold of that. It's all I had to hang on to."

Burgen remarks, "One of the biggest problems in America is the disintegration of the family. 60 percent of marriages today will end in divorce. Why's that?" In Chad's words, "The absence of God. He is the key factor in keeping any relationship together. When I get married, Jesus is going to be first." Mark chuckles as he says, "The guys in the band make fun of me and call me Richie Cunningham." "Oh, yeah, well my family is like 'LEAVE IT TO BEAVER,'" adds Chad.

Rachel states emphatically, "Right now I can say I'm not gonna get divorced!" "It's not gonna be in my vocabulary, either," proclaims Scotia.

issue #5
Please Notice Me

Homosexuality, bisexuality, straight, pierced and tattooed. "There are people who do things for attention, while others do things like piercing or tattooing just because they think it's cool," explains Will. Scotia shares, "I remember as a child piercing my ear myself. I do think there are some areas in which we can challenge our parents—and have our own identity."

David reacts, "I think it's important for each person to have his or her own identity, but I believe it can be taken to an extreme." Seven souls talk about their own identity and those of their friends.

issue #6
Facing Our Prejudice

At 12:30 a.m. we arrived at an in-store event at John's Bookshop in Wheaton, Il. The JEDI movie caused us to be late for AudioA's autograph party. Bob Herdman hadn't gone to the movie so he was already at the bookstore. Steven Curtis Chapman, who had been patiently waiting with Bob, muttered something about "Audio Delinquent."

This discussion was prompted by our inner-city tour of Chicago, our visit with the homeless people living under a bridge and our drive through Cabrini Green earlier in the day. The talk brought out some intense conflict and went into the wee hours of the morning as we closed the bookstore.

issue #7
Sex: Enough Said

How far is too far? We sat in an empty hot tub (fully clothed) in the Mall of America in Minneapolis. We talked about sex, dating and our criteria for marriage.

"I won't date anyone I know who's not a Christian, because you can just go crazy," says Vicki. "I want somebody who's going to challenge me and encourage me in my relationship with Jesus. A big attraction is to look at a man of God who makes me want to worship God even more," explains Lisa.

So what about witnessing to someone while you're dating? "It worked for me. My wife wasn't a Christian when I met her," says Will. "We were friends first, and I was telling her about the Lord. I came to a point when I said, 'I can't date you because you're not going to know the love I know—because I know God, the Creator of love.'" Come along for a candid look at relationships.

Sunday, March 9
- Met up in Nashville, Tennessee
- Entrance interviews at the airport
- Dinner with Audio Adrenaline and record label execs at San Antonio Taco Co.
- Laser tag
- Ice cream at Baskin-Robbins
- Crashed at Ben's house

Monday, March 10
- Lunch at Barbwire's Steakhouse
- Nashville Speedway U.S.A.
- Bongo Java
- Cool Springs Galleria food court
- Go-carts, video games and movies

Tuesday, March 11
- Road trip to Indy
- Lunch at Market Square Arena
- Wonder if Michael Jordan ever showered in this locker room?
- Steamed veggies and curried chicken
- Show time
- Backstage with SCC

Wednesday, March 12
- Truck stop, Plaza 109 Gas Grill
- ZZZ . . .
- Day off in Columbus, Ohio
- Lunch at the French Market
- Hittin' the links at the Airport Municipal Golf Course
- Dinner at Damon's
- Bowling

Thursday, March 13
- Interview at Horizons Film and Video
- Dinner at the venue
- Show at Battelle Hall
- Buses roll to Chicago

Friday, March 14
- 2:00 a.m. stop at DQ
- Lunch at Rosemont Horizon
- Inner-city tour of Chicago
- Under the bridge
- First-class catering
- Center stage
- RETURN OF THE JEDI opening night

Saturday, March 15
- On to Minneapolis
- Lunch and showers at the Target Center
- Mall of America
- Hot tub sex talk
- Half-dying/bleach party in AudioA's dressing room
- Performing "Big House" on stage
- Pizza and prayer on the bus
- Long journey home

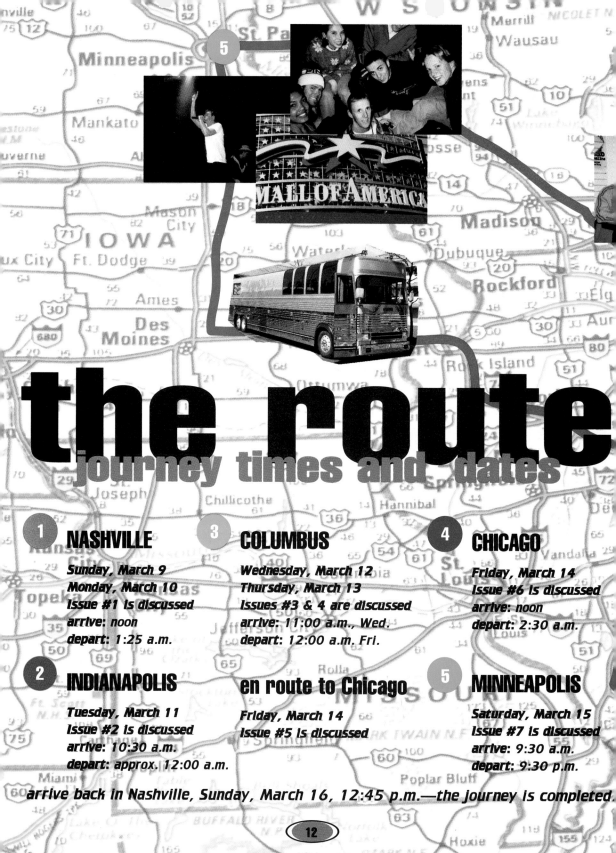

the route
journey times and dates

1 NASHVILLE

Sunday, March 9
Monday, March 10
Issue #1 is discussed
arrive: noon
depart: 1:25 a.m.

2 INDIANAPOLIS

Tuesday, March 11
Issue #2 is discussed
arrive: 10:30 a.m.
depart: approx. 12:00 a.m.

3 COLUMBUS

Wednesday, March 12
Thursday, March 13
Issues #3 & 4 are discussed
arrive: 11:00 a.m., Wed.
depart: 12:00 a.m. Fri.

en route to Chicago

Friday, March 14
Issue #5 is discussed

4 CHICAGO

Friday, March 14
Issue #6 is discussed
arrive: noon
depart: 2:30 a.m.

5 MINNEAPOLIS

Saturday, March 15
Issue #7 is discussed
arrive: 9:30 a.m.
depart: 9:30 p.m.

arrive back in Nashville, Sunday, March 16, 12:45 p.m.—the journey is completed.

IC0313 SEC 54 C 6 A 24.50

24.5¢ FLOOR

SEC 54   * SIGNS OF LIFE TOUR *
             * STEVEN CURTIS CHAPMAN *
       1)   WITH SPECIAL GUEST
       C   * AUDIO ADRENALINE *
             BATTELLE HALL @ C.C.C.
021FEB   THU MAR 13 1997 7:30 PM

AUDIO ADRENALINE RACING

Lisa Sampson

Born: 9/12/75
Age: 22
Hometown: Born and raised in Huntington Beach, California

Education: Attends Southern California College, studying psychology, with a minor in Spanish
Career aspirations: "I would like to work interculturally in the social field, get my master's and Ph.D.; I want to build others up emotionally and show them that true fulfillment in life is only found in Christ."
Future goal: "Go to every country in the world before I die."
Job: Waitress at an Italian restaurant—Amaci Trattoria
Role model: "My mother is a strong devoted Christian with a huge heart. She's a conqueror."
Words to live by: "I love passion for life. That's one thing that draws me to dancing, because I can be passionate in that."

John Whitton

Born: 12/26/78
Age: 18
Hometown: Mission Viej[o] California

Education: Attends Saddleback University
Career aspirations: Film director, cinematographer
Job: Graphics director for Metropolis Productions in Orange County, California
Words to live by: "I can always have fun in any situation and wish everyone else could feel the same way.

Rachel Eichenberger

Born: 12/20/77
Age: 19
Hometown: Cincinnati, Ohio, although she spent most of her life in Springfield, Illinois
Education: Attends Anderson University
Career aspirations: "I plan on studying English and history, and maybe be some kind of writer."
Job: Sales associate at Berean Christian Store
Little-known fact: "In the sixth grade, I did a science project on sailboats with my friend Laura. We thought it was the best project ever, but it wasn't very good at all."

Born: 10/10/78 **CHAD ANGONE**
Age: 19

Hometown: Littleton, Colorado
Education: Attends University of Northern Colorado
Career aspirations: A computer-related field,
missions or music
Job: Baker at Einstein's Bagels. "My favorite bagel
is cinnamon raisin."
Role model: "One of my youth group leaders, Erik Dixon."
Little-known fact: "I write my own songs on the piano."

Born: 10/21/76 **Scotia Little**
Age: 21

Hometown: Bowie, Maryland, right outside of D.C.
Education: Bowie State University
Career aspirations: "I want to go into full-time vocational ministry,
working with youth. I also aspire to do some writing."
Job: Tutoring Spanish and working as an RA (resident assistant)
in her dorm
Role model: Ruth in the Old Testament
Little-known fact: "I've had over a dozen addresses."

David Lissitt
Born: 10/6/79
Age: 18

Hometown: Dallas, Texas
Education: Highland Park High School
Career aspirations: "Wherever God takes me—
possibly a Christian singer or performer."
Job: Referee for YMCA games
Role model: "My dad, and John Woodell."

Victoria Laine
Born: 10/13/76
Age: 21
Hometown: Danville, California
Education: Attends Diablo Valley College
Career aspirations: Actress (drama, as opposed to comedy),
non-fiction writer or elementary teacher
Job: Baby-sitter/nanny

S COACH CO.. IN
USDOT 582467

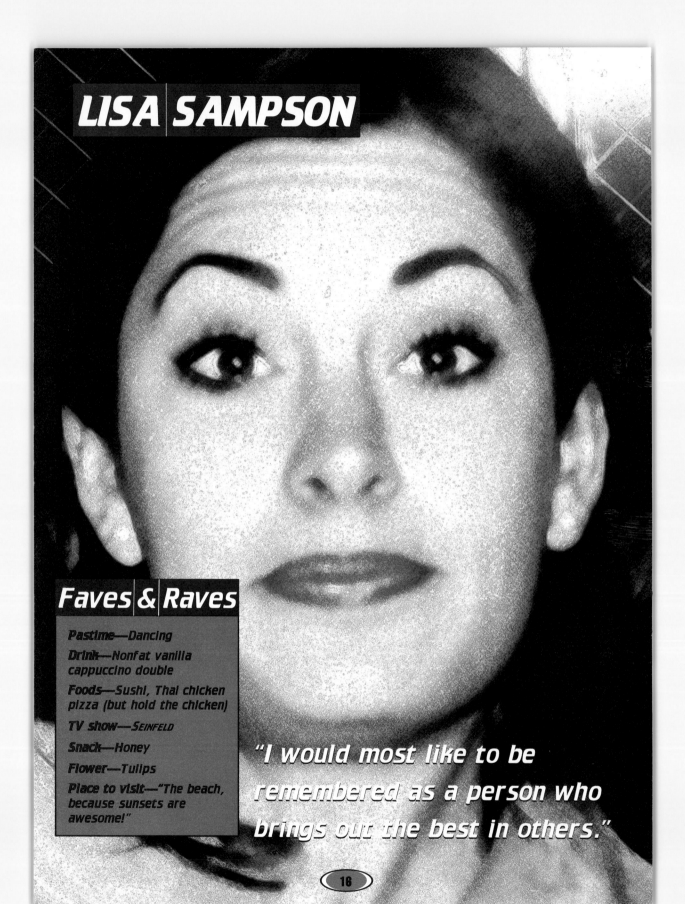

LISA SAMPSON

Faves & Raves

Pastime—Dancing

Drink—Nonfat vanilla cappuccino double

Foods—Sushi, Thai chicken pizza (but hold the chicken)

TV show—*SEINFELD*

Snack—Honey

Flower—Tulips

Place to visit—"The beach, because sunsets are awesome!"

"I would most like to be remembered as a person who brings out the best in others."

16

1 boating is a favorite memory I have of my brother and me

2 pretending to be a "fish." I always loved the water

3 Christmas with my domestic reindeer

4 sharing a "bonding moment" with my mom

5 with one of my best friends, my cousin Carla

6 enjoying African dancing with the native Ghanian people

More About Lisa

Hi, I'm Lisa. I live in Huntington Beach, California. I work and go to school. I enjoy running, exercise, waterskiing and snowboarding. I love the unfamiliar—people and places. Our family pets include a dog, two cats, two birds, two tropical fish and a bunch of goldfish.

I've been a Christian my whole life. I've been on a lot of mission trips to Brazil, Ghana, Amsterdam, England, China, Japan, Korea, Hong Kong and Indonesia—all with "Kings' Kids" through YWAM (Youth With a Mission). I was 11 years old when I started participating in these trips through dancing, singing and drama.

Every single culture has something unique to offer. I've gained a wide range of experiences on these various trips. I've worked with prostitutes on the streets, discipled people and helped with first aid. One of the two biggest experiences that I remember was in Ghana. I was 18, and I had just graduated from high school. That was the first trip when I really stepped out to share the Lord. I learned to be content with God. Like David demonstrates in the Psalms, I know that even if I don't ever feel God, hear or see him, I'm going to believe him. God has filled an emptiness inside me that has made me whole and given me purpose. I've tasted what is not of God and I know I don't want it! Right now, God is teaching me consistency. He is also teaching me not to cling on to emotion, but to hang on to his promises—taking the Bible as his Word and knowing its truth.

I hope whatever I do will make a positive difference in someone else's life. I know God has a plan for me and I'm not going to settle for anything less than his best.

18

JOHN WHITTON

Faves & Raves

Hobbies— Collecting records and toys (He brought Woody from TOY STORY and MegaMouth on the trip!)

Foods—Vegetables

Movies—FARGO, HUNCHBACK OF NOTRE DAME (Disney version)

Cartoon character he's most like—Shaggy from SCOOBY DOO (Charlie Brown runs a close second)

Place to visit—My room

"I do not want to be remembered for my career or any materialistic success I achieve."

1	age 3
2	age 5
3	age 15 with friends
4	at Ben's place
5	Lisa, Vic and I at the Waffle House experience

March 9, 1997

As I got off the plane, I was greeted and being filmed. Then we got to meet everybody, which was cool. Everybody is really nice and not very intimidating. —Chad

March 11, 1997

I think people that are closed-minded about things in life are missing out on opportunities to understand different kinds of people, cultures, ideas and experiences. —John

March 12, 1997

The bus is plush. I am enjoying myself. There are moments, but that's to be expected. I don't have super connections with the people. I can relate to John the most. —Vicki

My name's John. I wasn't really into high school. Everyone in my school was really into cliques.

I'm a vegetarian, primarily because of animal rights.

I am from a strong Christian family. I've never really gotten into the Christian thing and I've never really understood it. My life doesn't exactly show that I'm a Christian. My life is fine the way it is going now; it's not bad. But, sometimes I think it messes people up.

I think what I experienced at Christian camps was more of an illusion. When you go home, it's not the same. I have strong convictions, but they may not be from God, but rather from my family. God is definitely out there and I'm over here. I don't know if he is real—there's never been anything that's proved it to me.

If someone asked me, "Are you a Christian?" I'd say yes. I'm very self-motivated. I know I won't lose my salvation, but he's not the main driving force. When people say, "Just give it to God," I don't understand what they mean.

I enjoy movies, especially new releases. We saw a few movies during the trip. I suggested that everyone go to see "Return of the Jedi" on opening night, while we were in Chicago. Sixteen or 17 of us, including AudioA, piled in a van and drove to the theater after their concert. Bob was the only AudioA member who didn't catch the flick. The movie lasted longer than we expected so Bob, Steven Curtis Chapman and Carolyn Arends went to the autograph signing at John's Bookshop without us. When we arrived, people were waiting on autographs. During the ride back from the movie, I kept hearing Mark say, "We're in big trouble." Scott Brickell, AudioA's manager, runs a tight ship. He was a little steamed, but he got over it once we finally arrived. Plenty of fans were still waiting for AudioA.

Faves & Raves

Pastimes—Piano and art

Food—Chicken salad sandwiches

TV shows—ER and PARTY OF FIVE

Musical group or artist—Sarah Masen, Seven Day Jesus, Dime Store Prophets and Steven Curtis Chapman

AudioA songs—"People Like Me," "Man of God" and "Walk on Water"

Scripture—2 Corinthians 3:4-6, 18

Place to visit—Springfield, Illinois

Cartoon character she's most like—"It's a cross between Piglet and Tigger."

"I want to be re... someone who ... abundantly fo... trite, but it's ...

1 my first driving lesson

2 me (with the "pippi" braids) and my sister

3 eighth grade graduation

4 I've always loved fall—it's my favorite season

5 3 years old and "blooming"

6 on the trip in Columbus OH

7 my friend Dani & I right before we cut our hair

Rachel

n Cincinnati, Ohio. If
live at home but
reassuring me about
me now—God was
ed to be there. I
who's 16 years old.
ve grown up in the
Christian schools,

on a Bible study
al relationship with
t Christianity is not
re in relationship
I believe God
through other people.
sheltered or not, but
o come on this trip
e a great experi-
way from work and
leave that behind
ad. I've never

ger household and I
othes. I like doing
nt to do public rela-
type of advertising.
nt to be a writer?
w. Always add
irst. Check the pock-
't want to wash a
se you will have lint
thing. When I'm
do laundry. Do I
get married? Maybe.
to, but I also want
a career. I like
dryer sheets
ther than adding
abric softener while
'm washing. That's
ll of the laundry
sson for now. You
an catch the dryer
cle later.

March 11, 1997

I think Rachel is
very kind and
straight-ruled.
She's scared to
take a step over
the boundary. She
has a good heart
and is sincere.
It's obvious that
we come from
completely differ-
ent backgrounds
and experiences.
-John

March 13, 1997

Rachel and I were
in the same hotel
room. I'm soooo
glad. Later in the
day, I felt sick to
my stomach and
she was a very
calm presence. We
talked about guys
and her anger.
She's really
hurting. -Scotia

March 10, 1997

Lord, I want to
hunger and thirst
for You . . .
Lord, please give
me that hunger.
Spirit, please
intercede and
pray the things I
need to know and
pray. Prepare me
to be used howev-
er You want on
this trip. I marvel
at the fact that
I was chosen. . .
It's all You God,
not me. Please
help me keep in
step with You.
-Rachel

CHAD ANGONE

"I would like to be remembered by my love for God."

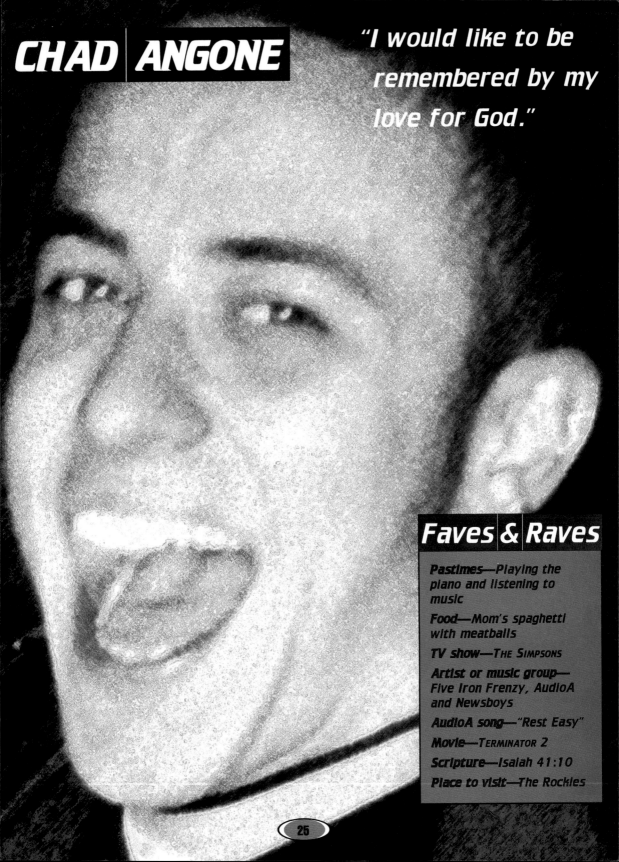

Faves & Raves

Pastimes—Playing the piano and listening to music

Food—Mom's spaghetti with meatballs

TV show—THE SIMPSONS

Artist or music group—Five Iron Frenzy, AudioA and Newsboys

AudioA song—"Rest Easy"

Movie—TERMINATOR 2

Scripture—Isaiah 41:10

Place to visit—The Rockies

1   as a baby being cute

2   as a baby being really cute

3   playing golf with Matt, Mark and Scotia

4   with my best friend, Mandy

5   in the back yard doing nothing really important

6   with my awesome red hair and my dog, Buddy

March 9, 1997

We arrived in Nashville. The first night we stayed at Ben's (AudioA's drummer) house. We got into deep and honest conversations about our backgrounds. It was kind of weird for me because of the questions that I had to answer about my artificial leg. But, I'm fine talking about it and pretty comfortable with it. But, people I hardly knew were asking really personal questions about my leg. We found out a lot about everyone. It was an exciting, tiring day. P.S. Ben had the sickest shower and bathroom. It was covered in dirt and mold. That boy needs Mr. Clean. —Chad

March 11, 1997

Chad is committed 24-7. He is not one person on tape, and another off. He is a good leader and he stands behind what he believes. -John

WHAT'S UP? MY NAME IS CHAD. I live in Denver, Colorado with my parents and younger brother, Paul. We have two dogs, Buddy and Boujo.

My dad's a minister. He pastors the church we attend and it is going very well. I always try to be aware and not judge other people, but love them. That is the best example that I can give them. That's what we are about (as Christians), and that's what God is about. If people approach me and ask questions, I am all for it because I love sharing Christ with others.

A lot of people ask me about my prosthetic leg. It came up right away on the trip. The people at the airport weren't very sensitive and it was a pain to deal with. My peers on the trip seemed genuinely interested in knowing about it. I was born without a femur bone, and without a knee. At age 10, I had an operation, and now I have a prosthetic leg. I can just take it on and off, and it doesn't really slow me down that much.

I don't feel very self-conscious about it at all. God has always taken care of my needs. In Exodus, when God called Moses to free his people in Egypt, he told him he had given all that he needed. And, I'm like, "Yeah, God." I'd rather people just ask about it than stare.

I have a great group of friends in Denver and I love them very much.

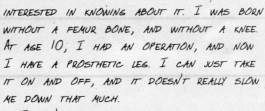

"ONE OF THE ISSUES THAT I'VE HAD TO DEAL WITH RECENTLY IS HOMOSEXUALITY. It really hit home for me because one of my childhood friends told me that he is gay. I've known him forever. My mom used to baby-sit for him. He called me several months ago and said, 'Chad, I have something to tell you.' I expected him to tell me that he had a really great class or something, but he told me that he is gay. He has a boyfriend. I had a hard time with it, but I know God has control of the situation and he has control of homosexuals in our society. He's still King of this world we are in. I told my friend that I don't agree with homosexuality at all. I don't condone it or support it, but I'll still love him the same. I still love the guy to death. God's working through it and God is doing good things."

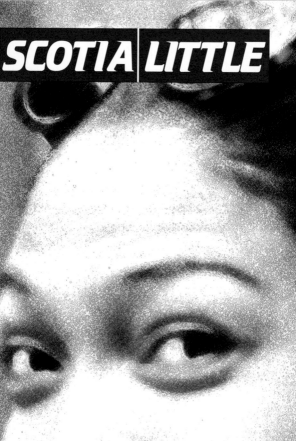

SCOTIA|LITTLE

1	in the 3rd grade, one of those awkward years when your head is bigger than the rest of your body
2	sleeping at Papa's (my grandfather's) house at age 4
3	in the 1st grade—I'm not smiling because I had no teeth!
4	writing in my journal on the bus
5	coming home from ballet at age 4—still one of my greatest loves
6	practicing my karate kicks

SCOTIA

March 9, 1997

It was an emotional parting at the airport. I really miss Vincent. I've been wondering what he is doing while out of the country. Is he safe? Does he miss me too? I cried this morning. I rode on the plane between two crazy, funny men. I didn't know who would be picking me up at the airport. Ben, from AudioA, met me at the gate. He's cool, really down to earth. -Scotia

March 9, 1997

Long story short—the whole crew came together and we went out to eat. We met the rest of the band at the San Antonio Taco Company in downtown Nashville. Cool folks, no bloated heads. It took me a while to realize that I was the only person of color . . . felt a little out of place when everyone was talking about music and different groups, because I don't listen to their kind of music. I listen to Christian reggae, rap and black gospel groups. -Scotia

March 11, 1997

I think Scotia's great. I really like her. She is very strong, and I admire anyone who is strong in what they believe in—no matter what it is. I love her a lot. Nothing is going to break her. -John

March 13, 1997

I was explaining to Scotia that recently I have felt the importance of being totally genuine, real: not a fake Christian. I can quote Scripture, and Sunday-school answers and even formulate answers that I don't truly feel—just so I can have an answer. -Rachel

DAVID LIGGITT

"I'd like to be remembered as a man who loved Christ and lived his life as a committed Christian."

1. my younger years. even now I still look goofy!

2. I can't believe my mom sent this picture! nice ears!!

3. baseball . . . a sport I never mastered

4. my little bro., William, and I posing for a Kamp pic

5. my best friend Lauren and me at Kanakuk kamp in Missouri. we like to get funky

6. I think I saw a ghost!

7. I look like a snowman! This was in Minn.—I was freezing

March 9, 1997

Today was crazy! Thoughts coming into the trip included me being nervous. I had never before come into a situation not knowing anyone. Well, today I was made comfortable. It is interesting getting to know one another.
-David

March 11, 1997

Dave's a nice guy, but I personally think he got hung up on the fact that he ran over a raccoon with a car because it was going to bite him? . . . After the fact that he chased it. -John

I play offensive receiver and defensive back on my high school football team and I'm a member of Fellowship For Christian Athletes. I'm also in student council.

I am involved in K-Life (a form of Young Life) and I've attended five summers at Camp Kanakuk in Lampe, Missouri.

I grew up in a Christian home. I have three brothers, ages, 14, 20 and 21 and we have a dalmatian named Smokey. I accepted Jesus into my heart when I was six or seven years old, but I really don't think I realized the meaning of Jesus' death on the cross until I was about 12 or 13. I didn't really start walking with God and having a quiet time until then. In my life, God has blessed me so much, it's unexplainable.

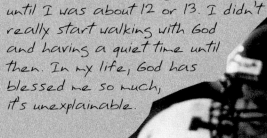

"ONE ISSUE THAT IS A BIG PROBLEM IN MY HIGH SCHOOL IS ALCOHOL— I think it's a problem everywhere. My choice has been not to drink and I have stuck with that. They say that the best way not to sin is to be away from the sin. That's why I think it's really important where you find yourself on a Friday or Saturday night. With drinking, it's so much easier not to worry about having it right there, rather than having it be right next to you—then making the decision. One time I was at a place where there was alcohol and I was out of there in about five minutes. I feel like so much is riding on my high school career and I don't want to ruin it, just because of drinking."

VICTORIA LAINE

Faves & Raves

Pastimes—Running, reading, drinking coffee (favorite flavor—espresso)

Foods—Japanese food, sushi, cheese

Favorite Scripture—John 19:30

Artist or music group—Ani DiFranco, Counting Crows

Movie—DEAD MAN WALKING

Pet—Black lab named Sparky

Place to visit—"Boston, because my grandparents live there"

"I want people to remember me for being real."

34

1 Where it all began

2 my birthday

3 outside my Laurel ave. apt.

4 back in the day, cheerleading

5 Simone and I in "The Hollywood"

6 a call home to find a ride

7 (I think I was feeling weird that day). I don't know what was up

More About Vicki

Hi. I'm Vicki. I'm from San Francisco. I've done drugs. When I was 15, I got pregnant and had an abortion. I've been through hell and back. I have a hard time with who I am—I feel like I'm not clean.

I know God loves me, but I don't know. Sometimes he slaps me in the face and says, "Wake up, Vic." I don't think God thinks good things about me. I've never wanted to commit suicide, because I love life. A lot of it has to do with my past. Some of the things I saw when I was little I shouldn't have been exposed to. I guess I don't feel like I'm loved.

Currently I don't do drugs, but I do drink some, and I smoke some. I blame my parents, straight-up. My parents' divorce really [ticks] me off. It all comes back to the fact that I don't have a dad. I get really jealous of others who have a dad. I don't put God in the Father role at all.

March 9, 1997

The guys we met in AudioA are cool. I am here and it's totally God—I acknowledge that. I really like everyone who is here. -Vicki

March 9, 1997

I am feeling good about things. I've shared a lot already. I really want to be understood, heard and listened to. I don't want to be lectured to or looked at like I'm some kind of freak. -Vicki

March 10, 1997

The movie we saw tonight really hit me. It makes me so angry about how destructive parents can be to their children. The main character in the movie had such a beautiful heart, so full with a yearning for love, yet—was cheated out of life. It was so unjust. I especially feel that way about Vicki. She is greatly suffering the consequences [of her past]. -Lisa

March 11, 1997

I don't know what is going on with her. I can't say that I understand what she is all about. I like her, but I can't figure her out. -John

36

Will McGinniss

Birthday: February 25

Hometown: Marion, Ohio

Education: Studied elementary education at Kentucky Christian College for five years. "I dropped out because of the direction God was taking me through AudioA."

Career aspirations: "I would like to own an extreme adventure sports store. It would be a place that also takes trips to mountain expeditions."

Job: Bassist, Audio Adrenaline

Cartoon character he's most like: Droopy Dog

Role model: Billy Graham

Favorite nail polish colors: Blue-black and manic panic

Quote: "I don't want to be remembered for anything in me, but for some of the things that I stood for—that I was a man of integrity, encouragement, compassion and love—the attributes that Christ showed."

Ben Cissell

Birthday: August 14

Hometown: St. Louis, Missouri

Career aspirations: "I would like to be a youth minister someday, get married and have lots of kids."

Job: Drummer, Audio Adrenaline

Role model: "My Grandpa Seabaugh, because he's a good Christian and everybody likes him."

Little-known fact: "All my life, I've never wanted to be a drummer; I always wanted to be a professional soccer player."

Cartoon character he's most like: Shaggy from Scooby Doo. "I don't know why. Maybe because he's tall, lanky and stupid."

Quote: "There's a song by Blues Traveler called 'A Hundred Years.' It's written from the perspective of someone who is not saved. In the song, they say that whatever you're doing in life won't mean a thing in 100 years. But, I think what we're doing will matter!"

Bob Herdman

Birthday: March 8

Hometown: Lynchburg, Ohio

Education: Kentucky Christian College

Career aspirations: "I'd like to help my wife, Jeanette, who's just started working on a record deal. (Her musical style is pop rock.) I would also like to start doing more songwriting for other artists."

Job: Keyboards, guitar and vocals, Audio Adrenaline

Role model: Simon Peter

Cartoon character he's most like: "Bugs Bunny, because he's smart. He's always cool, calm and nothing shakes him."

Quote: "I would most like to be remembered as someone who is joyous."

Mark Stuart

Birthday: April 14

Hometown: Owensboro, Kentucky

Education: Graduated from Kentucky Christian College with a degree in education

Career aspirations: "I'd like to do mission work at some point in my life, maybe work with my parents. My family served in Haiti for four years."

Job: Vocalist, Audio Adrenaline

Role model: "It would be too scary to be like Jesus. It would be cool to live your life like Billy Graham. He is a radical guy even though he is viewed as a conservative in the world. Also, my dad is a warrior. He's got the heart of a servant and he knows the Bible inside and out."

Little-known fact: "I played drums in high school for different groups. My brother David used to sing better than me—he still does."

Cartoon character he's most like: Shaggy from SCOOBY DOO. "I think I look like him. My grandma and my mom think so too."

MARK STUART
Lead Vocals

"Bad things are gonna happen, but it's not because God is making them happen. I know that he is about loving his children."

40

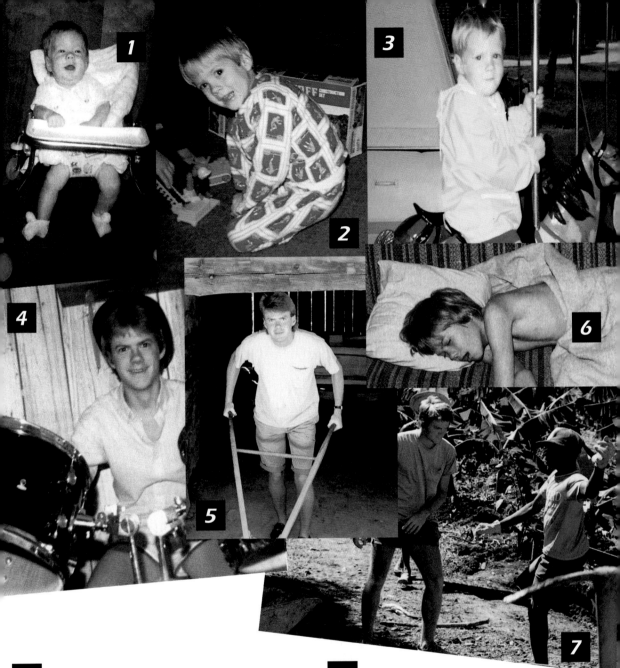

1 about 8 or 9 mos. old	**4** my ambition to be a great drummer
2 my favorite construction set	**5** life on the farm (Cade's Cove Great Smokey's)
3 vacation in the Smokey's	**6** my favorite hobby—then and now
	7 life on the mission field (in Haiti 1987)

More About Mark

I was born in Owensboro, Kentucky

and my dad still pastors a church just outside of that town. I have a younger sister, Kelly, and an older brother, David. I think it's the easiest to be the middle kid.

My parents and my sister have been involved in mission work in Haiti. They lived there while I was in college. My sister got leukemia while they were serving the Lord in Haiti and they moved back to the United States. Now, she's completely cured. [I believe that] ultimately God is the Creator of the world and is in control.

My family will probably continue to be involved in mission work. I also have a desire to be involved in missions work at some point in my life. I really fell in love with that kind of work—it's adventurous. Unlike what we do, you have the opportunity to see the fruits of what you're doing. We go into a city and we are gone the next day. Mission work is really hands-on and you work with kids. You not only save lives every day, by giving them food or medicine, you also have the opportunity to share the gospel. It is very rewarding, though very hard, work.

I went to college at Kentucky Christian College (KCC) and majored in secondary education. I can teach physics, calculus and chemistry. I don't think that's what the Lord's calling me to do, but I did enjoy it. I went through that degree because I planned on going to the Air Force Academy and I needed a science and math background. Originally, I was going to pursue aeronautical engineering and wanted to transfer after attending one year at KCC. I ended up staying in that program and finishing, because we started playing music together our freshman year . . . Barry Blair, Bill, my brother and me.

I was in a lot of bands in junior high and high school. I was always in a band, but never in a Christian band. When we started playing at KCC, it just took off and I felt like that's what God wanted me to do.

Fact: Grew up doing plays and musicals

Fact: "As a teen I didn't believe in myself enough and didn't trust God."

Fact: Married his wife, Kerri, in Las Vegas

Pets: Two German short-haired pointers, Vegas and Vienna

BOB HERDMAN
Rhythm Guitar

"Our audiences can expect fun, energetic stage shows. We try to have a joyous time as we present the message of Christ, a message of hope."

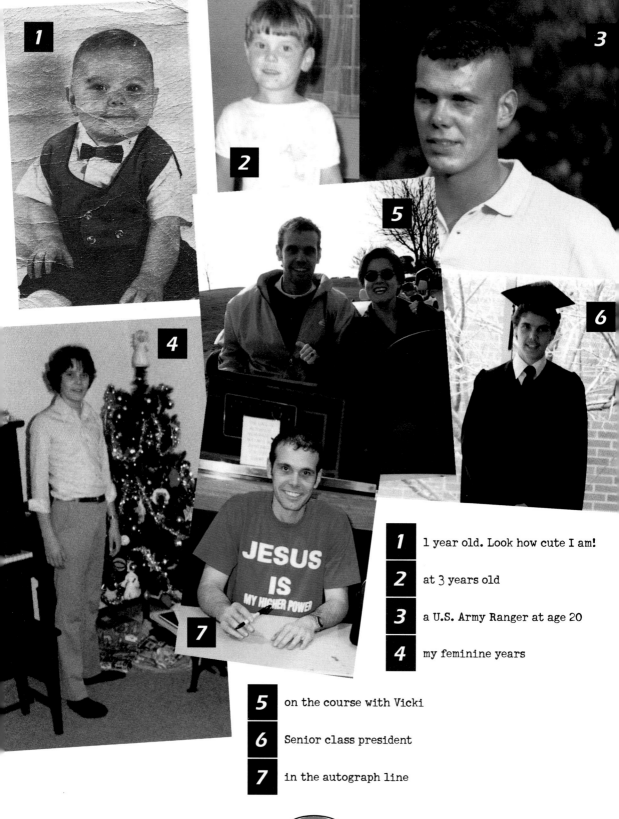

1   1 year old. Look how cute I am!

2   at 3 years old

3   a U.S. Army Ranger at age 20

4   my feminine years

5   on the course with Vicki

6   Senior class president

7   in the autograph line

More About Bob

I grew up listening to Christian music, like Petra. I wasn't allowed to listen to anything else. That's something I hope people will get from us, that they will listen to our music and say, "That's ours." They'll see that Audio Adrenaline's members are good guys, though we're not specifically an evangelical band.

One of the most spiritually challenging things that the band's had to learn this year is patience. When you're out on the road, sometimes it gets boring. We go on a roller coaster in terms of spirituality, like at times when you get away from your devotions and wonder why you're so miserable. When we have devotions, everyone is on a spiritual high. When you're with a whole group, it is almost like everyone is going through the same thing. We try to have Bible studies every day on the road, around 1:00 p.m. We help each other with the different struggles that we may each be facing. One of the most exciting things for me, within the band, is writing new songs. I get bored easily. It's fun to write new songs. I write the majority of the lyrics, but we all work together on the songwriting. In the past, I used to write all the lyrics, but it's coming together now where we all do a little bit of everything.

I think our biggest thing is to edify Christian kids and get them pumped up. That's what I've always seen as our focus, and I don't perceive it changing in the near future.

Fact: "I was nine years old when I became a Christian."

Fact: Married to Jeanette

Fact: They have one son, Waylen

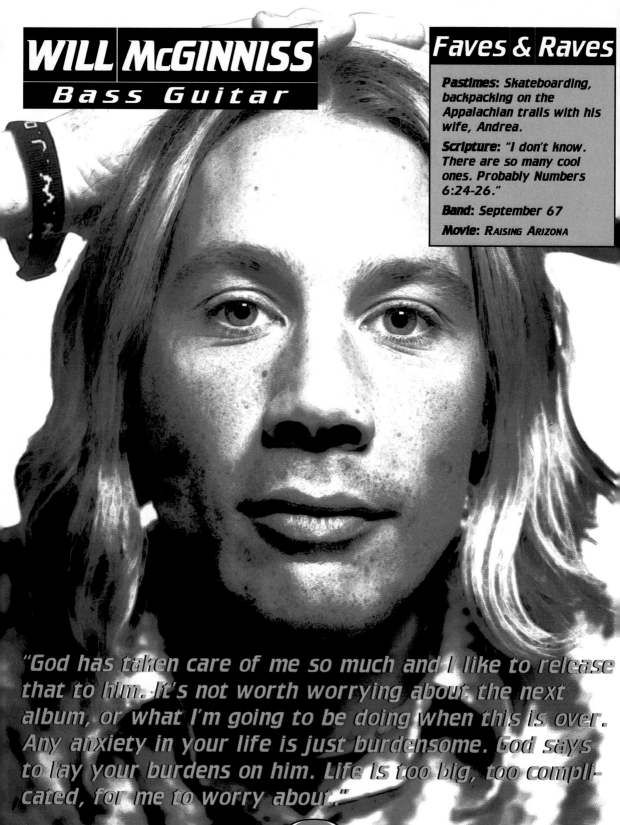

WILL McGINNISS
Bass Guitar

"God has taken care of me so much and I like to release that to him. It's not worth worrying about the next album, or what I'm going to be doing when this is over. Any anxiety in your life is just burdensome. God says to lay your burdens on him. Life is too big, too complicated, for me to worry about."

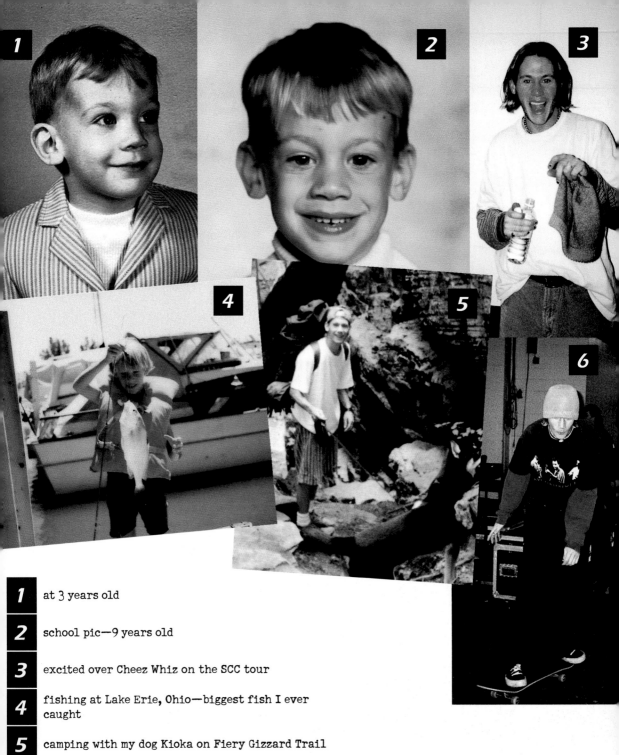

1 at 3 years old

2 school pic—9 years old

3 excited over Cheez Whiz on the SCC tour

4 fishing at Lake Erie, Ohio—biggest fish I ever caught

5 camping with my dog Kioka on Fiery Gizzard Trail

6 "a little pastime" on the SCC tour

More About Will

I was in the tenth grade when I became a Christian. At the time, I was the only one in my family. Eventually, my mom and my two sisters became Christians. I've seen God perform such great acts and miracles that I realize he's going to take care of me. I mean, he converted my whole family, and he is working in a mighty way.

My whole career has been a demonstration of me stepping out in faith. When I first went to college I thought I was going to be an elementary teacher. These guys approached me to be in their band but I didn't even know how to play an instrument. I really feel like we have a calling in Audio Adrenaline. When you give in to a calling, you see how big God can take it and what he can do through it.

I came from a broken family. I didn't have a father figure in my life. I really took hold of God being my "Abba" Father. My walk with him is really like hangin' with a best friend. You know that you can crawl up in his lap when things are not going good. Recently, my dad is becoming more open to God because of a situation in his own life, an illness that he has. I have had to step out in faith to ask God for the right words and just let the spirit work in me.

Fact: "I've been playing the bass guitar for over 11 years."

Fact: Married to Andrea

Pets: Two Siberian Huskies named Kioka and Jake

48

BEN CISSELL
Drums

"There's a lot of prejudging going on, not just with Christian bands, but in any art form. Before you listen to anyone else's opinion, I'd say check it out for yourself. Some people didn't like Picasso, some people didn't like Elvis Presley—now he's the king of rock 'n' roll."

1 1 year old—all about food!

2 when I was 3, I knocked out my teeth in a tricycle accident

3 soccer star of the Midfield Medina Rangers

4 shoveling snow at 15 years old

5 struttin' my stuff at senior prom

6 new drums at age 10

More About Ben

Fact: "I started playing with Audio Adrenaline on February 15, 1996."

Fact: "I like to look at old drums, or go to drum stores and see what they have. My set was custom designed in Nashville."

Fact: "Prior to Audio Adrenaline, I played in a lot of punk bands around St. Louis. I also played in jazz bands in high school and college."

Pet: A toy poodle named Péle

I try to relate to kids in a very real way. I'd like to say I trust God all the time, but I have trouble trusting anything. I'm just really hardheaded. After something good happens, I'll be like, Wow, God, that was cool! But, if anything isn't explained to me in black and white, I won't understand it. I'm always doing things wrong and it's kind of scary. I love this world. But sometimes all you hear about is the bad stuff. Everything that happens in this world, God is allowing it to happen.

God is directing my life. With the ministry that Audio Adrenaline has, we have the opportunity to share the gospel and to make a difference in people's lives. I feel like being around the other guys in the band is really a strong witness to me. I want to be that kind of example to other people.

Issue 1

"Hard to Handle"

Arrival times

David— 10:46 a.m.
from Dallas
Rachel— 12:00 p.m.
from Cincinnati
Chad— 2:51 p.m.
from Denver
Scotia— 2:55 p.m.
from Baltimore
Vicki— 2:57 p.m.
from San Francisco
John— 4:20 p.m.
from L.A.
Lisa— 4:20 p.m.
from L.A.

Sunday, March 9, 1997

2:00 p.m. Entrance interviews at Nashville International Airport

5:37 p.m. Dinner at San Antonio Taco Co. on 2nd Ave. with AudioA

7:08 p.m. Toured downtown Nashville

8:12 p.m. Played Laser Quest

9:21 p.m. Ice cream at Baskin-Robbins

10:48 p.m. Back to Ben's house where we all crashed

11:32 p.m. Issue #1—"Hard to Handle"

Monday, March 10, 1997

2:30 a.m. Sleeping bags never felt so good!

8:55 a.m. Lisa, Scotia and Vicki took an early morning walk around Ben's place

9:45 a.m. Up and showered

12:00 p.m. Lunch at Barbwire's Steakhouse

1:30 p.m. Nashville Speedway U.S.A.

3:12 p.m. Went to Bongo Java near Belmont University for some mocha, sweet tea and caramel creme coffee

4:06 p.m. Issue #1 continued in front of coffeehouse

6:45 p.m. Ate at the food court in Cool Springs Galleria, a mall in Brentwood

7:48 p.m. Go-carts and video games at Recreation World

9:35 p.m. Popcorn and a show at Galleria Cinemas

WE ALL STAYED AT BEN'S HOUSE ON SUNDAY NIGHT. HE LIVES WITH SEVERAL OTHER GUYS WHO ARE IN THE BAND *REALITY CHECK*. THEY are rarely home because of their touring schedules. The décor in the house had a definite '70s feel to it—a lot of gold and avocado green in the draperies and furniture. The bathrooms were grungy. They had plenty of food and drink and made us feel at home. We were all really tired—but looking forward to a great week! Sitting on the floor of the living room, we spent some time getting to know each other. It didn't take long for Vicki to lay her cards out on the table. The conversation centered around our diverse backgrounds and experiences. Thus, the journey begins.

Our talk so far has been good. [I believe] we need to stand up for what we think, even when someone says something that contradicts what we believe. We are being a little too nice still, but I'm sure it will rub off soon. — Lisa

AFTER WE PLAYED LASER TAG, WE GOT SOME ICE CREAM. AS THIS WAS GOING ON, WE WERE BEING FILMED . . . IT'S HARD TO ACT NATURAL AND NOT LOOK AT THE CAMERA. WE ALL WERE HONEST AND OUR CONVERSATION GOT REALLY DEEP. IT WAS KIND OF WEIRD FOR ME, BECAUSE ONE OF THE QUESTIONS I HAD TO ANSWER WAS ABOUT MY ARTIFICIAL LEG. — CHAD

We all played laser tag. It was a blast! I worked up a real sweat. By the time we were finished, I was so tired, I didn't know how much more I could take. We had a cool hard talk. I didn't even notice the camera. — Scotia

LASER QUEST

NICKNAMES

Chad — GravyTrain
David — Too Legit
John — PapaGeorge
Lisa — Shirley
Rachel — Laverne
Scotia — Scodiggity
Vicki — Venom

Ben — Ringo
Bob — Bob
Mark — Viper
Will — Ned

FYI: Viper was the big winner

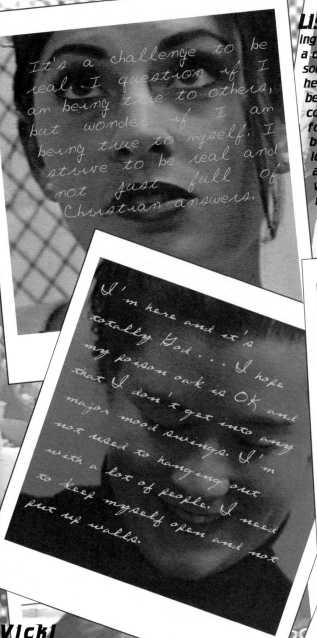

It's a challenge to be real. I question if I am being true to others, but wonder if I am being true to myself. I strive to be real and not just full of Christian answers.

Lisa attends school and is studying psychology. She wants to earn a degree and work in an intercultural field in some capacity. Long term, she really wants to help people grow into what God's created them to be. She's done a lot of traveling. She feels God continues to open doors as he reveals his plan for her life. Lisa says that a lot of students, both in high school and college, are searching for identity. They are trying to find out who they are. "I hope to encourage others to live out their values—to live out who they are and know why they are who they are. A lot of people compromise because of their friends or the various situations in which they find themselves."

I'm here and it's totally God... I hope my poison oak is OK and that I don't get into any major mood swings. I'm not used to hanging out with a lot of people. I need to keep myself open and not put up walls.

I think that people who are closed-minded about life are missing opportunities to understand different kinds of people, cultures and experiences.

Vicki

aspires to be an actress. She says that she admires Winona Ryder. One of her favorite movies is USUAL SUSPECTS. She believes that Gen X is speaking out and saying, "I want to be an individual, I want to be me and I want it my way—but it's going against what society says."

John's the youngest child in his family. He has an older brother and an older sister. He's into watching movies, producing films and hopes to pursue a career in that field. John feels that one of the main issues that high school students have to deal with today is peer pressure. "I'm not really this way, but a lot of people I see are trying to fit into a group—they will drop everything just to fit in. They become someone they're not almost overnight."

For a long time, a real love of mine has been music. I'm a member of the choir at Highland Park. I think it would be a neat experience to go on this tour for a week and set to see what it's like and if it's really what I want to do. God has done things in my life within the last year to show me that music should be a part of my life.

David loves playing football and attending summer camp. At Highland Park High School, he is a member of student council and is involved in Dallas K-Life. He's also active with the Fellowship of Christian Athletes and enjoys spending time with his girlfriend. His sense of humor is contagious. He says one of the major issues that people in high school deal with is alcoholism. "My choice has been not to drink and I've stuck with that. I think if you struggle with something, like drinking, it's best not to put yourself in a situation where you're exposed to it. It's better to stay away from it and then you won't be faced with the temptation."

I'm not an articulate speaker, but I wanted to be a part of this trip. Now that I'm here, I am questioning my own abilities. Apart from You, Lord, I can't do anything. Please help me to keep in step with You.

Rachel's a good listener. She's soft-spoken at first, but has a real interest in others. Her desire to grow closer to God is transparent. Rachel says her peers have to deal with alcohol, drugs, sex and depression. "You have to hit people with where they're at and these are some of the issues that need be dealt with. If you are able to talk to people and tell them why you believe what you believe, they might listen."

Jim Burgen has been the high school minister at Southeast Christian Church, in Louisville, KY, for seven years. His ministry involves some 500 students on a weekly basis. In addition, he is a sought-after speaker for national and state conventions, and youth conferences.

I WANTED TO BE A PART OF THIS AUDIO ADRENALINE TRIP BECAUSE IT PROVIDES AN OPPORTUNITY FOR MORE PEOPLE TO HEAR ABOUT CHRIST. I WANT TO CHANGE THE WORLD FOR JESUS, AND THIS IS ONE MORE STEP GOING FOR IT

I wanted to be a part of this trip because I have found a lot of cultural irrelevance in the youth ministry materials I have seen. I would like to add an African-American twist to this trip. I would like to bring the inner-city student's perspective to it. I want to be a part of helping people come to know Christ.

Chad's friendly and outgoing. It didn't take long to find out he always has a positive attitude and is generally in a good mood. He's a baker at Einstein's Bagels. The very first night of the trip, he was asked about his prosthetic leg. Chad says that one of the big issues that people in high school deal with is partying. "We had two kids die from our high school in a car accident and a kid died last year from a drinking-related accident. We're also doing drug searches now in our schools with K-9 units, so that's an issue. It's not just pot, it's heavy drugs and a lot of kids are involved in it." Why? To escape.

Scotia is studying psychology and plans to graduate from Bowie State University in December of '97. She's working to put herself through school and is considering the possibility of going to seminary to study ministry. "It's not by default that I want to go into ministry, but it's the only thing that I have a passion for." She grew up in a single-parent home, with her mother and brother. Jim Burgen asked her what she thought about racism. "I am an idealist and an optimist. I think the problem with racism begins with relationships. I can tell you or other black people all day long that you need to get rid of that attitude of racism in your heart. But, if people don't see it in my life, or that I am making an effort to form relationships with people from other cultures, they won't listen. It begins with one-on-one relationships and people reaching out to one another."

AUDIO ADRENALINE

bloom

AUDIO ADRENALINE RACING

AUDIO ADRENALINE sponsors the hood of a NASCAR. On Monday, after lunch at Barbwire's Steakhouse, one of the pit stops for the day was Nashville Speedway U.S.A. We saw the car and met the driver, Bam Dixon. He talked with us about the car and answered our questions. We sat down by the track and road pastor Jim Burgen broke the ice by asking us to share one of our most embarrassing moments.

I think it was my junior year. I had this cute skirt on with tights. After dance class, we got dressed in our regular clothes, and I got dressed quickly, because I had to get to the cafeteria before the line closed. I ran in there and noticed that several people were staring at me and laughing. Then my friend came up to me and said, "Your skirt is inside your tights."
— Scotia

It was Thanksgiving a couple of years ago. I was wearing baggy shorts. Everyone was asking why I wore "those things so low." My dad and I were washing dishes. He was trying to be funny as he pulled down my shorts, but he ripped down my boxers too! My whole family was there. I couldn't drop the dishes—there was nothing I could do to quickly pull them up. I was [ticked]! - John

It was my freshman year in high school. It was only the second week of school. I already had two tardies in one of my classes after lunch, and a few of my friends and I were running through the hall because we didn't want to be late. There were a lot of people waiting in the hall outside the class. When we were running, I didn't just fall, I did a total face plant and my lips touched the ground. There were tons of people around, so it was really embarrassing. I got up and went to class and recuperated. - Lisa

Mine was at one of our football games. I don't know what I did, but I tripped and caused about three guys to fall over me. There we were, on the 20-yard line, all falling down. - David

MY MOST EMBARRASSING MOMENT WAS AT MY OLD CHURCH. IT WAS THIS REALLY BIG CHURCH AND IT HAD THIS REALLY ADVANCED INTERCOM SYSTEM THROUGH ALL THE PHONES—THERE WAS A PHONE IN EVERY OFFICE AND IN EVERY ROOM. IT WAS ON SUNDAY, WHEN THE SERVICE WAS GOING ON, AND THERE WERE ALSO PHONES IN THE SANCTUARY. WELL, MY DAD WAS THE MINISTER AND WE WERE DOWN IN THE FELLOWSHIP HALL, WHILE HE WAS GIVING HIS SERMON (THERE ARE PHONES DOWN THERE TOO). MY FRIEND AND I WERE IN SIXTH GRADE. I PUSHED THE "ALL INTERCOM" BUTTON THAT GOES TO ALL THE PHONES. I WAS SCREAMING, "JUSTIN, JUSTIN, GET YOUR BUTT DOWN HERE!" EVERYONE CAME UP TO ME AFTER THE SERVICE AND ASKED WHY I HAD PUSHED THAT BUTTON. MY DAD HAD HEARD IT AND ANNOUNCED TO EVERYONE, "OH, THAT'S MY SON." I DIDN'T KNOW WHAT WAS GOING ON. SOME PEOPLE THOUGHT IT WAS A FIRE ALARM. ONE WHOLE SUNDAY SCHOOL CLASS LEFT THE BUILDING, SO MY DAD HAD TO TALK TO THEM. THEY WERE COOL ABOUT THE WHOLE THING, BUT EVERYBODY KNEW ME BECAUSE I WAS THE PASTOR'S SON. — CHAD

there and my parents argued over who was g
to get a divorce. That was a really hard time,
going on and we were wondering if somebody
and I didn't stop crying the whole night. It ha
to go to church. It was difficult, because we

ed. note: Rachel's parents didn't get divorced until jus

Jim asked, "Why would a God of love make
sees your priorities aren't focused on him, he
through hell, because he wants you to be so

"In hard times before I walked with God, it
have to get through this—I can't just lay dov
only way I knew to handle it was just to num
get overwhelmed. Sometimes it's hard for me
(I feel bad today). I didn't acknowledge it un
tried to seek fulfillment through a number o
realized I definitely needed to try God. Wher
back."

"Do you think you're afraid of it?" David a
get to you now? For me, it's easier to go thr
that people without God are afraid to deal v
want to?" "I think they deal with it the way
Scotia responded.

TODAY WAS A LOT OF FUN! I LOVED RIDING THE GO-CARTS AND PLAYING VIDEO GAMES AT RECREATION WORLD. I LOVE HANGING OUT WITH AUDIOA. THIS IS SO COOL. IT BLOWS MY MIND.

I don't relate much to any- one, except for Ben and Will from AudioA. My mind shuts off listening to someone, when they show signs of stupidity or express an egotistical outlook.

I'm surrounded by my peers. We were engaging in revealing and transparent conversations. Lord, You answered my prayer. You certainly revealed yourself to us, as we came with our lives, paths and stories. We laid them out

Denial is depression and when you suppress it, it can damage your emotions. What you are doing is allowing it to dwell there. I think people deal with situations in the best way they know how. Then, they find out the only way that's going to be long-lasting is through God. I don't know if some people are afraid and some people don't want to face it, but for whatever reason, it's the only way they know how to deal with it and survive." - Scotia

I think that's why I have such a hard time accepting God or his help, because I just trug through everything. I can just go through life, and I don't trip out. I can say that I have come to this point in my life and I am doing all right. - Vicki

I don't think that you should live your life to just get through, or just to get by. You should live life to the fullest and be successful in whatever you do. I don't think you can focus on getting by with Christ. If you have Christ in your life, you will enjoy life. Obviously, you're going to suffer and go through hardships, but life is something that has worth and value. - David

I definitely agree with that, but how can you communicate that to someone? We are talking this "Christianese" stuff and we're saying you need to be here, but people don't always know how to get from here to there. They need to be given some direction. It's like telling someone, "You have to be on top of that mountain," but they can barely walk, and we're not providing what they need to get there. We know what they need and we know what the Bible says, and we know we are supposed to have abundant life. We know that we are holy and chosen, but that doesn't address the issue of reaching people where they are.

How can we deal with people where they are, and take them where they need to be? It is the stuff in between that I really think is life-changing. I'm talking about Christians now; there are a lot of people who are living defeated lives. They need to understand what it means to walk with the Spirit, and what it really means to yield to him. Until you understand that it's his Spirit within you, and you were crucified with Christ you can't really comprehend that concept. But when you do understand that, then you can live victoriously. - Scotia

A person needs to be at a place where he acknowledges that he needs God. Even for the true Christians, who know the Spirit, who know the Bible . . . there are days when you feel like you can do it yourself; there are days when you fall on your face. That's what Jesus meant when he was saying it has to be all day, all the time. People can't do it without God. Jesus didn't promise that life would be without pain. Pain is the thing that polishes. I don't have a problem with pain, but it is how you deal with it. The important thing is to deal with it through God, to go to him and say, "I need your help." Some people try to cope with it by being a workaholic and working themselves to death, or being sexually active and being lost in relationships, or putting someone on a pedestal, by worshiping a man or a woman. If you deal with life in those ways, your relationship with Christ is going to suffer, because it's secondary to how you're dealing with your feelings. You need to say, "God, I can't do this without you." That's not just the beginning—it's everything. The bottom line is how we deal with God. You can numb yourself for a couple of years, or for 20 years, but the issue is still inside of you. What you did was push it away, hide it, put it in an archive, but it's still there. The only way to heal the pain is to let God deal with it. – Lisa

think it's just humbling yourself before God and knowing you can't do it without him. I don't think a non-believer can come to Christ before he realizes that there's no other way. – David

Like John said last night, when you give it to God, what does that mean? You give it to God when there's nothing else to do—it's either God or you're going to die. — Jim

It's surrendering, complete surrendering, when you think of a battle. You realize you're being defeated, but you've been trying for so long to fight and you just keep on getting killed, wounded—you're just holding on. And finally you realize you need to surrender. You need God to take over. – Lisa

Maybe that's what it means to be crucified with Christ.

— Jim

Over and over, everyone's said the answer was "I gave it to God and everything was OK." That's the simple answer everyone always has. My mom always says, "Oh, you should pray about it." But, people who don't understand Christianity are just sitting there saying, "Well, OK. . . ." It just seems like a false sense of security to me. - John

How do you work through your problems, then? - David

If I have a depression problem or whatever, I usually think it out and say, "OK, I did the best in that situation that I could." I don't usually make decisions that I'm not 100 percent happy with. If I do, I'll know what not to do the next time. Then, I have that reassurance, if the situation comes up again, that I'll know how to handle it. - John

You've never had anything knock you so hard, flat on your face, that you had to say, "I need God"? - Scotia

I've had bad things happen, like suicidal friends. I get caught up in the middle of helping them. If they have a big problem, they come to me and I help them out.
But, when I have a problem, I have nowhere to go. But, I get through it. - John

When your friends come to you for help, what do you tell them? I know a lot of my friends come to me for advice. I don't always know what background they come from, but I usually tell them to talk to God and see what he says-if you want to call that giving it to God or whatever. What do you say to them? - David

It depends on the situation, it depends on what they're going through, and how I can help them. Everyone has a different situation. Sometimes I give them a different perspective, a different light on how to look at the situation. - John

Does God Care

about the problem of pain?

"Praise be to the Lord, to God our Savior, who daily bears our burdens. Our God is a God who saves; from the Sovereign LORD comes escape from death." Psalm 68:19, 20 NIV "My flesh and my heart may fail, but God is the strength of my heart and my portion forever." Psalm: 73:26 NIV "I've told you all this so that trusting me, you will be unshakable and assured, deeply at peace. In this godless world you will continue to experience difficulties. But take heart! I've conquered the world." John 16:33 THE MESSAGE "Cast all your anxiety on him because he cares for you." 1 Peter 5:7 NIV

People of all ages struggle to cope with pain and difficulties. Every day in this country: 1,000 teenagers take their first drink of alcohol, 500 use a controlled substance for the first time, 2,200 teens drop out of high school and 6 teens commit suicide.

"The only way to heal the pain is to let God deal with it." — Lisa

2

Issue

"Black and White in a Gray World"

"About one third of our generation doesn't care about anything important. It's kind of like 'anything goes.' We feel like everything's changing, and we have nothing to do with it, so we'll just sit back and

This is one person's view about what Gen X thinks about absolutes. But we don't all agree. In this issue, we set out to discuss our struggles, our temptations—and absolutes.

let it happen. We have nothing stable to grasp. No one to look up to. No one to believe in. No one to trust but ourselves," said one 17-year-old male, in a recent quote that appeared in PARADE magazine.

Tuesday, March 11, 1997

12:30 a.m. Let's go Krogering!

1:25 a.m. Sendoff with Eddie DeGarmo, VP of A & R for ForeFront Communications—AudioA's record label

1:55 a.m. Everyone found a bunk—wheels roll to Indianapolis

2:52 a.m. All asleep to the humming of the bus

9:30 a.m. Up already?

9:47 a.m. "What kind of cereal did we buy?"

10:30 a.m. Showered backstage at Market Square Arena, home of the Indiana Pacers

12:00 p.m. Lunch in catering area

1:30 p.m. All access passes and tour of venue

3:00 p.m. Issue #2—"Black and White in a Gray World" in dressing room

6:00 p.m. Chinese night—steamed veggies and curried chicken. Quick glimpse of Steven Curtis Chapman

6:02 p.m. AudioA's sound check

7:30 p.m. Show starts

10:30 p.m. Autograph signing

11:30 p.m. SCC visits us after the show

Audio Adrenaline
ALL ACCESS
DREW BACA
LIGHTING DIRECTOR

We met Darrell, the driver of the bus we would call home for the next few days. AudioA kept commenting about how cool our bus was. (It's a lot newer than theirs.) This 1996 Prevost was equipped with two VCRs, sound systems, CD and cassette players, microwave, refrigerator and a bathroom. Only one problem with the bathroom—no solid waste allowed.

The stage crew is huge, with at least 50 people. The stage, sound system and lights quickly took shape, with the exception of one casualty. While the crew was unloading equipment, one of the bus driver's ankles got run over by a forklift. He was rushed to the hospital. Later that night, he was OK and back at the venue.

The locker room showers weren't ideal, but it was refreshing to clean up after an all-night sleep on the bus. During the afternoon, we toured the venue and helped the roadies unload equipment. Eating lunch in the catering area at the venue is always an adventure. Food—there's always a variety, but you never really know quite what to expect!

After the concert

we were sitting in the locker room, waiting to meet Steven Curtis Chapman. We talked about what we were going to do to greet him.

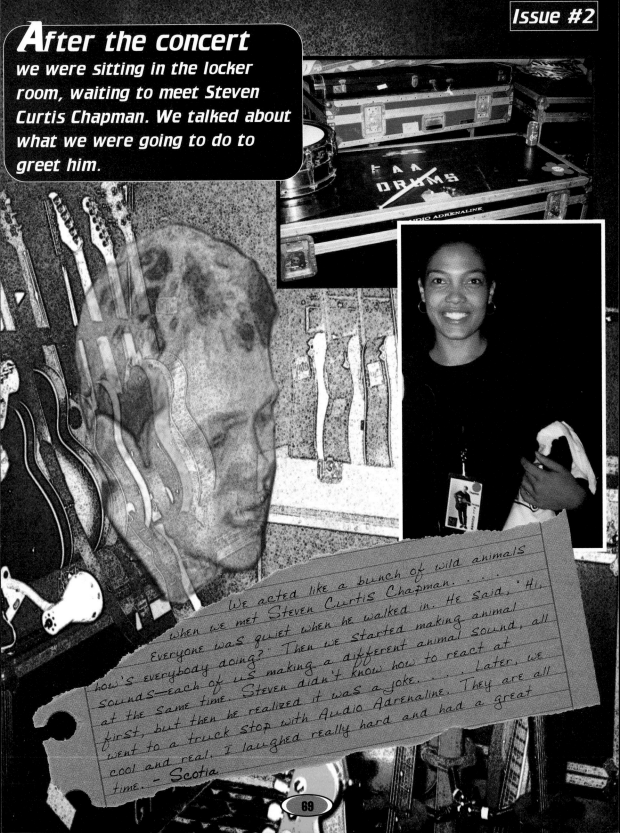

We acted like a bunch of wild animals when we met Steven Curtis Chapman. . . . Everyone was quiet when he walked in. He said, "Hi, how's everybody doing?" Then we started making animal sounds—each of us making a different animal sound, all at the same time. Steven didn't know how to react at first, but then he realized it was a joke. . . . Later, we went to a truck stop with Audio Adrenaline. They are all cool and real. I laughed really hard and had a great time. – Scotia

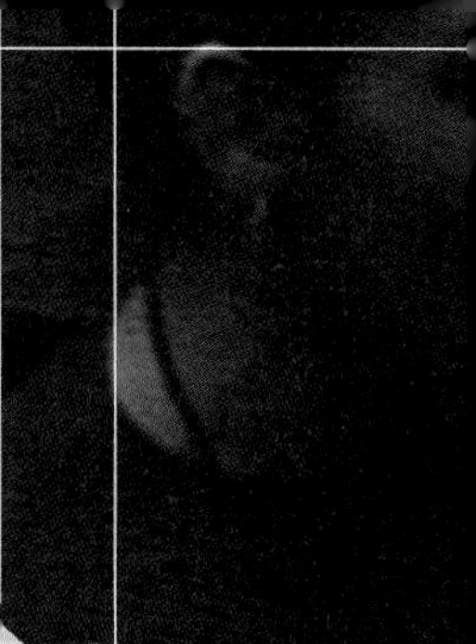

s us to hate
the truth or
grace, but we
However, we c
say, "God, I ha
ant to do thi
ercome this." -

I HAVE A FRIEND WHO IS A HOMOSEXUAL. — CHAD

Can you be gay and be a Christian? — Jim

THE BIBLE SAYS A MAN SHOULD NOT LIE WITH A MAN AND A WOMAN SHOULDN'T LIE WITH A WOMAN, BUT MY FRIEND DOESN'T BUY INTO THIS—HE RATIONALIZES. . . . . I TRULY BELIEVE THAT MY GAY FRIEND IS SAVED. YOU CAN'T SAY HE'S NOT SAVED, BECAUSE EVERY SIN IS THE SAME. — CHAD

We don't want to sin, but it's still our nature. - David

I also have a friend at school who's gay. She's an amazing student; her grade point average is 4.0. When I found out she was gay, it didn't make me stay away from her. Jesus said, "It's not the healthy who need a doctor, but the sick." In the Bible, Paul illustrates this scenario. He was trying to be a good person by keeping the law. In his own strength, he was ultimately defeated by the problem of sin. He had good intentions, though he attempted to win the battle with sin by his own plan and ability. He said in Romans 7:19, 20 that he still struggles with sin: "For what I do is not the good I want to do; no, the evil I do not want to do—this I keep on doing. Now if I do what I do not want to do, it is no longer I who do it, but the sin living in me that does it." - Scotia

I think the Bible definitely sets up absolutes. There is a right and a wrong. If everybody has his or her own morality, eventually there is nothing to go by. There is no way to the Father except through Jesus Christ, is an absolute. . . . I think homosexuality is wrong. The Bible says it is wrong. Jesus never really talks about it too much, but Paul talks about it in Romans. - Mark

I think we need to be careful. Some Christians live in a prideful state all the time, but you don't hear people saying, "Oh, they're not saved." But, we do that in other areas. If we deal with homosexuality that way, then we better do that with bitterness and deceit—and everything else.

It's up to the Holy Spirit to convict people of sin—it's not our job. God can deal with it in his time. His kindness leads us to repentance. . . . Homosexuals already think that Christians aren't very loving. We need to show them the love of Christ. Otherwise, we're hypocrites. – Scotia

If you're not struggling with sin, I would really question whether or not you're humble before God. – David

As Christians, we are called to fix our eyes on Jesus all the time. Satan is smart, man, because he knows where to hit us. We need to be awake and feed ourselves with the Word and prayer and good relationships. When thoughts come in, we need to take those to God immediately, because if we don't, that's when we compromise. We are all weak. – Lisa

When I lived in West Hollywood, I had really good times with my friends. But I would bring some of these bad thoughts before God. I won't even go there, because I have an addictive personality and I know what it would do to me. – Vicki

A lot of churches just do not know what is going on. They spend too much time rallying themselves together, being self-centered, rather than reaching out to those who need help. – Scotia

When it comes to sin, tolerance comes to mind. It's very hip right now to be tolerant of everything. It sounds really Christian at first, but at the same time, we can't be tolerant of the fact that these people might be living in sin. [Sometimes we need] to show tough love.

We live in a bubble on a tour bus. The majority of the people running the tour are Christians. We're not exactly in the real world. Let's say I was teaching school and standing for what I believe. I'm sure I'd be called intolerant. - Mark

I think a really big issue right now is intolerance. What we call "conviction," the world will call "intolerance." If someone says to me, "you're intolerant," I think I don't want to be classified as intolerant. We should be intolerant to a degree-we should be intolerant of sin, but we should still love the sinner. I think there's a fine line. The world is distorting that, trying to make it look bad. It's not bad, it's right—it's conviction. We should be convicted about what we believe and what God says. If that's what intolerance is, then call me that. Intolerance is a politically incorrect word. - Bob

I can't see him, but I know Jesus Christ is here. We're not always given all the facts, but we still have to trust God. He is the absolute! - Mark

We need to get out of our comfort zones. God commanded us to love and we have to put that love into action. — Scotia

We can't change people, but God can. Jesus loved people not just by saying, "I love you," but by doing it. If we let Jesus do the work in their hearts, then God can reach them. People will come to Christ when we jump out of our comfort zones. We need to wake up in the morning and ask, "Lord, where can you use me today?" When you see someone walking on the street, you can either stop, or you can choose to walk on by. I look for people who are hanging out by themselves. — **Lisa**

At one point

in the discussion, we got off the subject. During the conversation, as Rachel was trying to explain something, Vicki replied, "I'm just tired of all this bulls**t."

Jim: "Does that [swearing] offend anyone?"

Scotia: "Yes."

Vicki: "Do you really think Jesus would say, 'Your swearing is offending me'?"

Everyone: "Yes."

Vicki: "I don't think that would come into play with Jesus and me."

Lisa: "Why is that?"

Vicki: "'Cause it's not about swearing—it's about love!"

Jim: "I'm not saying that you're going to Hell for using the 'f' word. I'm just saying that it's inappropriate for this setting."

Vicki: "See, that just throws the whole Christianity thing off for me."

Scotia: "Vicki, my love for you doesn't have anything to do with what you do; it has to do with Jesus' love for you—and I love you because of that."

Vicki: "But it's between me and God!"

Jim: "I want us to work together. If I have a problem, or whatever, we have to work it out. You can't just walk away and say God and I are going to work it out."

Vicki: "For me, cussing is not an issue I need to work on right now."

Scotia: "If you don't think it's a problem, why are you so upset about what I said about your cursing offending me?"

Vicki: "Because I take it as a personal attack. That f***ing [ticked] me off!!"

Scotia: "We do care about you, but we're still going to call you on things. The only personal thing about you being a Christian is your decision to accept Christ; other than that it is public—we're the body of Christ."

David: "We all want to become friends and we don't want to tear each other down."

Vicki: "My attitude coming on this trip was just to be myself. . . . . I swear. So what?!"

Lisa: "We do have to share things and hold each other accountable, that's when it becomes [our responsibility]. I love you, period."

(Visibly upset, Vicki got up and left the room.)

Chad: "Do you think she's mad at us, or what?"

Jim: "God can use her in great ways. She has a great heart—it's just covered up right now. Do you guys think I handled it wrong?"

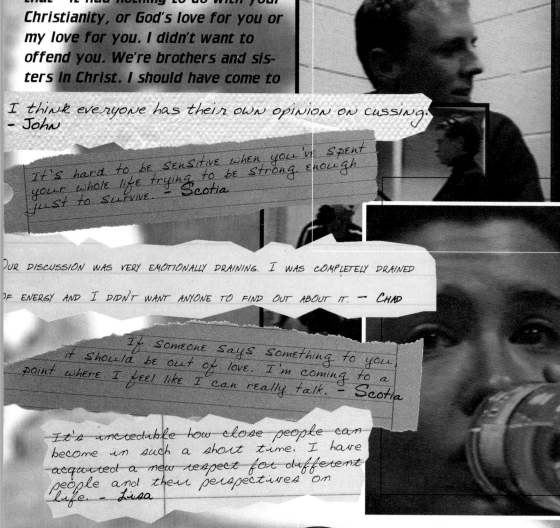

Rachel: "No, I think she looks at us like we're just fake. Every [time I] say something, I feel like I have to defend it. She's also taking it [like] it's a whole body of people against her."

John: "Well, it seems like there's five of you against us two—who believe diffe[rently."]

Scotia: "I just think some things should be said off camera. I'm trying to buil[d rela]tionships, and it's not impressive to come across with the Bible as the ultimate answer, or to come off preachy to someone."

Chad: "I always try to go to the Bible because it's the source of what I believe."

After Vicki came back in the locker room, Jim looked at her and said, "I was wrong to call you out in front of everyone. I apologize for that—it had nothing to do with your Christianity, or God's love for you or my love for you. I didn't want to offend you. We're brothers and sisters in Christ. I should have come to

I think everyone has their own opinion on cussing. - John

It's hard to be sensitive when you've spent your whole life trying to be strong enough just to survive. - Scotia

Our discussion was very emotionally draining. I was completely drained of energy and I didn't want anyone to find out about it. — Chad

If someone says something to you, it should be out of love. I'm coming to a point where I feel like I can really talk. - Scotia

It's incredible how close people can become in such a short time. I have acquired a new respect for different people and their perspectives on life. - Lisa

you in private. I didn't mean for it to be a personal attack."

Scotia: "If you're in a relationship, like marriage, your husband might offend you or do something to hurt your feelings. But, if it was me, I would tell him it hurt my feelings, but that doesn't mean I didn't still love him or would stop loving him. . . . Vicki, I'm sorry if it seemed like a personal attack."

Jim brought some closure to this issue by saying, "In these talks, I really want to understand all of you. Sometimes that means asking, 'What's going on inside of you?' It's not saying what you should or shouldn't do—it's just [to get a better] understanding."

Vicki: "I don't believe it. I hear it [that you love me], but I don't actually take it to heart. Obviously, I care—or I wouldn't be a wreck right now."

David: "I know you have certain things you want to get rid of—you told us."

Vicki: "I don't think it's unconditional love."

Chad: "With us, or with him [God]?"

Vicki: "With everybody. If it's a relationship with God, he's not telling me to stop swearing."

Scotia: "Just because I don't feel comfortable with your cussing, doesn't mean that I don't love you. I do love you. It means that I want you to be the best that God created you to be."

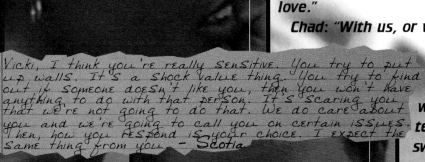

Vicki, I think you're really sensitive. You try to put up walls. It's a shock value thing. You try to find out if someone doesn't like you, then you won't have anything to do with that person. It's scaring you that we're not going to do that. We do care about you and we're going to call you on certain issues. Then, how you respond is your choice. I expect the same thing from you. - Scotia

I can't say I understand what's going on with Vicki, or what she is about. I like her, but I can't figure her out. (I can't think of anything we have in common.) However, I think Vicki and I relate to each other more, because we live in the real world. - John

Some Kind of Zombie

ust have been confused or ...in to let th

vil in my brain.

rd, did I enjoy the change that you ma

inside my heart?

, here they come though I'm not afraid

here's no temptation I can't evade.

stand up straight, I look through the ha

begin to walk through the maze.

ere they come, they're all upon me,

ut I'm dead to sin like some kind of zom

horus

I hear you speak and I obey,

(Some kind of zombie)

I walk away from the grave,

(Some kind of zom

I will never be a

(Some kind of zor

I give my life away.

People can see through us.
They sense if we are sincere in
what we believe. — Rachel

What does God think

about absolutes, sin and grace?

"When they kept on questioning him, he straightened up and said to them, 'If any one of you is without sin, let him be the first to throw a stone at her.' . . . 'Then neither do I condemn you,' Jesus declared. 'Go now and leave your life of sin.'" John 8:7, 11 NIV "Jesus answered, 'I am the way and the truth and the life. No one comes to the Father except through me.'" John 14:6 NIV "I do not understand what I do. For what I want to do I do not do, but what I hate I do. . . . .Now if I do what I do not want to do, it is no longer I who do it, but it is sin living in me that does it." Romans 7:15, 20 NIV "Therefore, there is now no condemnation for those who are in Christ Jesus, because through Christ Jesus the law of the Spirit of life set me free from the law of sin and death." Romans 8:1, 2 NIV "He doesn't treat us as our sins deserve, nor pay us back in full for our wrongs. As high as heaven is over the earth, so strong is his love to those who fear him. And as far as sunrise is from sunset, he has separated us from our sins." Psalm 103:10-12 THE MESSAGE

In America today, 72% of all people do not believe in absolute truth. Even in the church, 59% of all churchgoers do not believe that there are absolute rights and wrongs. In fact, 45% of active church youth believe that lying is sometimes necessary.

"We need to help one another. The only personal thing about you being a Christian is your decision to accept Christ; other than that it is public— we're the body of Christ."
— Scotia

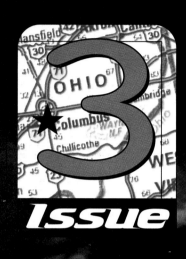

3

Issue

"The Church: Hospital or Country Club?"

Wednesday, March 12, 1997

12:55 a.m. Truck (bus) stop at Plaza 109 Gas Grill

2:45 a.m. All asleep on the bus

11:00 a.m. Woke up in Columbus, OH and checked into Cross Country Inn

12:00 p.m. Lunch at the French Market

1:25 p.m. Hittin' the links at Airport Municipal Golf Course

6:55 p.m. Dinner at Damon's Ribs (Day off for the band—no show tonight; Will spent the day in Marion, OH with his family.)

7:25 p.m. Where's the Imodium?

9:00 p.m. Issue #3 at Capri Bowling Alley with Bob, Ben and Mark

11:45 p.m. Late night movie in John's room

"We're starting to realize that Audio Adrenaline's lifestyle is hard work. Life on the road is demanding. The days and nights can be long, though you have the opportunity to have fun. You also have the opportunity to learn a lot, see different things and meet interesting people in each city." — **Chad**

"After we left the venue, we stopped for food. The restaurant was more like a greasy spoon, and not too fancy. They also had a general store, which carried a little of everything you could want—from food and supplies to novelty items and gifts." — **Rachel**

"The Gas Grill gave a few of us a stomachache. Jim and I got sick from the truck stop the night before. I kept asking everyone how to cure diarrhea." — **Scotla**

81

After we checked into our motel and ate lunch, we headed to the Airport Municipal Golf course for nine holes of golf. It was a nice day, however, 90 percent of us had never golfed before. It was an adventure. David tried to kill himself and others by driving his cart into a tree. — Jim

I've never gone golfing before. It was cold, but it was fun being on a team with Chad, Mark and Matt. I learned how to golf and was actually pretty good by the time we finished the game. - Scotia

Golf today was frustrating. I felt as if I was a burden to my team members. I was frustrated, because I was so bad. My feelings were a reaffirmation of how I have felt out of place and not accepted on this trip. I am not the cool, popular kid and I never have been. - Rachel

I heard that we are golfing today. Great! I hate golf. - Vicki

Today has been tons of fun. We hung out at the nearest mall, ate lunch at our favorite places within the food court (with the exception of Vicki, John and Lisa, who walked across the street to Waffle House), played video games and then, we all went to play golf. Golfing was the best! The other people on my team were Mark, Matt (the retail man) and Scotia. Matt is an awesome guy and getting to know him was really fun. It was also awesome hanging out with Mark. It seemed like he was paying special attention to me, which I loved! — Chad

After a messy dinner of ribs, we went to Capri Bowling Alley. Jim began by asking, "What would high school or college students find, if they came to your church?" Rachel responded, "I think a lot of people are looking for a relationship with God, but they won't necessarily come to church."

"The other day, Scotia said that we should focus on going out and witnessing to other people. I agree with that. We need to bring people into the church, but I don't think we put enough emphasis on reaching out to people. Nonbelievers don't want to get out of their comfort zones and I think when you witness to them you get out of your comfort zone and that way you can help them," David said.

Bob jumped in and related something that had just happened to him: "I was talking with our waitress today. I know she didn't feel comfortable in the church. She said she grew up in a Christian home and she knew about some Christian music. She went on to say that she felt Christianity was forced upon her and she didn't believe in organized religion."

Lisa took the discussion and made it personal: "I don't want people to think that just because someone is a Christian that they are flawless and have all the answers. I know I am struggling and finding my way through the grayness of life, like everyone else. I question things, I doubt, I fail, compromise and I fall. I'm not proud of who I am. There are many times I look in the mirror and I don't like what I see."

"I want these bowling shoes."
— Chad

"How many people want brushed suede, multicolored shoes?" —Lisa

"How many people have worn these shoes? It's gross to think about it." — Scotia

Does the church judge you based on your appearance?

—Jim

I believe that the church family is cool, but at a lot of churches I see, there seems to be prejudging going on. After I became a Christian and I went into a church, a lot of people were like, "What is he doing up there playing drums to my kids?" It's like, "Isn't that the guy that blah, blah, blah?" It really bothers some people if you walk into church with long hair or have two earrings. – Ben

Do you feel prejudged walking into church? – Mark

Oh yeah, people stare, or just walk by and keep quiet. – Ben

How do you want to be treated? Do you want them to come up and hug you? — Jim

I don't want them to talk behind my back or think [negative] thoughts. I know you can't take someone's thoughts away like "What's he doing here?" – Ben

The church should be a place where the doors are open to everybody. If the church is not doing that, then they are not doing their job. Jesus accepted everybody, no matter what they looked like. It shouldn't matter. – Lisa

How should the church respond to someone's appearance? — Jim

I think they need to treat all people like they are normal and disregard what they look like. – Ben

What about a 70 year old? He doesn't see things the same way you do. Have you really felt like you have been judged based on your appearance? — Jim

Yeah, but I grew up in a pretty conservative church. The churches in Nashville aren't like that. – Ben

What's different within various churches? — Jim

It might be from where I grew up, but I don't get the whole thing of dressing up on Sunday—what about just being yourself? I don't get it. – Ben

I don't think you should be dictated by what the older people think. You should be more concerned about introducing people to Christ than making older people happy with the way you look. I don't think you should support traditionalism or whatever, if that's the way you dress, if that's the way you feel. I think there's a point when you should respect your elders. But, really, the job of the church is to meet people's needs, feed the hungry and introduce people to Christ.
- Mark

It might have a lot to do with the vision. There are very few churches in California that would look down on you because of how you dress. I lived in the Midwest and there are churches that believe how things have always been done is the way they should continue to be done; anything that's different, they look down on. - Lisa

"After dinner, we went bowling. I was so tired, I didn't think I would have fun. I woke up once we got started, and I bowled a pretty good game. We talked about the church, and whether we felt the church is demonstrating love and welcoming all people. We also addressed whether we feel the church is doing a good job of meeting the needs of young people. Ben spoke up and said he didn't always feel welcome (in the church) because of the way he dresses."
— Scotia

What if a young lady comes and is just beginning to understand Christ? I would rather she come to church, than worry about whether or not she is dressed appropriately. Then, after she has been coming for awhile, an older woman needs to take that young lady aside and form a relationship with her. - Scotia

A COUPLE OF MONTHS AGO, I HAD RED HAIR AND WAS KIND OF SCARY LOOKING. MY FATHER'S THE PASTOR OF THE CHURCH I ATTEND. SOME PEOPLE DIDN'T THINK IT WAS THAT BIG OF A DEAL, BUT OTHERS SAID, "YOUR DAD'S A PASTOR AND YOU NEED TO SHOW RESPECT." LOTS OF OTHER PEOPLE CAME TO ME AND THEY DIDN'T KNOW MY DAD WAS A PASTOR; THEY TREATED ME COMPLETELY DIFFERENT. — CHAD

What about presenting your best to God? —Jim

If you should present your best to God 24 hours a day, seven days a week; you should always dress up for him, not just on Sundays. — Ben

What if grandma needs you to, in order for her to worship? — Jim

I don't care what people think about me. It should be between God and me—that's it. - Vicki

IF I AM A STRONG BELIEVER AND SOMEONE HAS A PROBLEM WITH THE WAY I LOOK, OR WITH SOMETHING I AM DOING, I NEED TO RESPECT THAT PERSON, BECAUSE WE ARE CALLED TO NOT BE A STUMBLING BLOCK TO OTHERS. — CHAD

Where do you draw the line with what other people think? — Jim

Yeah, but when do you try to fix the problem? If someone came to me and said they had a problem with something like an earring, I would address that person by saying, "This earring has nothing to do with my belief in God." - Mark

I would ask someone why he or she has a problem with the way I look. - Vicki

Who sets the standards within the church?
—Jim

If you have been a Christian awhile, and you know there are believers who are offended by what you wear to church, I think there are times when respect needs to be taken into consideration. I do feel that churches need to be less concerned with the way people look. At what point do you say, "You know what, church isn't about wearing a nice tie and nice slacks—it's more about introducing people to Christ." I know it's that way on the West Coast, and there are a lot of churches in the Midwest like that too. People wear jeans at the church I attend and I feel comfortable wearing jeans. Maybe, if I was younger, I would feel more insecure about the way I look. - Mark

There does need to be a point when someone sets the standard. I've been in church when other girls have worn really short skirts—it's a stumbling block to me, let alone my brothers in Christ. - Scotia

Which is worse, that someone comes and offends people by what he or she wears or the person doesn't come at all? — Jim

CHURCHES ARE SUPPOSED TO BE MORE LIKE A HOSPITAL FOR THE SICK, FOR PEOPLE WHO NEED IT, NOT ONLY FOR THE FELLOWSHIP OF CHRIST, BUT WE'RE SUPPOSED TO WELCOME ANYBODY. LOOK AT THE BIBLE—JESUS HELPED THE PROSTITUTES, LEPERS OR ANYBODY—AND THEY WEREN'T DRESSED UP! — CHAD

I agree with that. At some point you have to stand up and teach people certain truths. First of all, we have to address it and say, "Can we talk about it? Why do you have a problem with it?" We have to deal with it and show respect. - Mark

WE ARE CALLED TO IMITATE CHRIST. EVERYONE IS WELCOME IN THE CHURCH. — CHAD

What's the real issue?
—Jim

Shouldn't our main focus in church be on worshiping God?
- David

Let's say they do worship God and that's their ultimate goal, but you are someone who is distracting them. Out of respect, then I would say put them first. I would still talk to them about the way I felt and what the truth is. - Mark

Who is the more intolerant, older people or students? — Jim

I think the ratio is about equal. Just as older people can be intolerant, I think young people can be as intolerant or selfish. - Mark

Older people are intolerant, which makes kids and even myself, be more rebellious. You say, "Well I'm going to show them. I'm going to do what I please." - Ben

It's kind of like, don't touch the wet paint - Bob

I remember one time when someone approached me about wearing pants to church. It was 20 degrees outside. I said, "I'm not wearing a dress for anybody."
- Scotia

I think you need to make waves. I don't mean to cause quarrels, but I do think the church has become very stagnant because of traditionalism. When I say make waves, I mean to think the way the New Testament church is set up. They didn't even have a church building. The way that we go to church is a concept that we have come up with over the past 2000 years. They used to meet in people's houses and sell their belongings and give the money to the poor. I think young people should always push people toward breaking their tradition, not for the sake of being rebellious, but to keep Christianity moving forward, so we don't get set in our ways. When I'm 40, I will probably look at 20-year-olds and say, "What are those kids doing?" But I also know what it feels like to be a 20-year-old. Don't be afraid to set an example for older people in the areas of faith.

— Mark

Is the church relevant to your life? When you consider the topics, style of illustrations or curriculum— is it relevant, or is it dated? If so, how can it be better?

— Jim

For me, it comes down to the preacher—there are some preachers that you walk away saying, "Wow, I got a lot out of that." But, at some churches I'll be totally blank, but my grandfather will say, "Wow, I got a lot out of that." - Ben

If you were reaching out to people who were just like you in high school or college, designing a service to reach them, what would you do? — **Jim**

It would be tough. I would start out by welcoming them and work on building a relationship with them. First, show them love. - Ben

It doesn't have to be anything so serious at first, just have fun and show them that you care. Have a good time and show them that you love them. - Bob

When we were in college, Bob used to come back to the dorm freaked out about youth ministry. He would take his kids to Pizza Hut and they would go and sit at another table. - Mark

I was a good youth minister, but my kids didn't know it. -Bob

Structure and planning are important, but I think one of the key factors is letting the Holy Spirit work through the situation. — Chad

One thing we have to remember, like Paul said, was that he became all things to all people so that he might save some. We need to go to the "gang bangers" and talk to them, and we also need to be able to go to the kids in Beverly Hills and talk with them in a relevant way. We need to be relevant to people. — Scotia

I think a big problem with the church is straight-up hypocrisy. — Mark

Do you think there are that many hypocrites? Is everybody on a big kick of looking for hypocrites? — Bob

We all have these different sins that we don't talk about from the pulpit, or from the stage or on our records. Let's just be honest—Jesus came here for the sick and the dying, not for us to act perfect and wear our nice suits to church. — Mark

What does God think
about the church?

"It is not the healthy who need a doctor, but the sick. But go and learn what this means: "I desire mercy, not sacrifice." For I have not come to call the righteous, but sinners."" Matthew 9:12, 13 NIV

". . . we are like the various parts of a human body. Each part gets its meaning from the body as a whole, not the other way around. The body we're talking about is Christ's body of chosen people. Each of us finds our meaning and function as a part of his body." Romans 12:4, 5 NIV "Even though I am free of the demands and expectations of everyone, I have voluntarily become a servant to any and all in order to reach a wide range of people: religious, nonreligious, meticulous moralists, loose-living immoralists, the defeated, the demoralized— whoever. I didn't take on their way of life. I kept my bearings in Christ—but I entered their world and tried to experience things from their point of view." 1 Corinthians 9:19-21 THE MESSAGE

Of the 82% of Americans who claim to be "Christian," less than half attend a local church on a regular basis. Only one-third of 18-30 year olds attend church. An estimated 97% of all church ministries are directed toward believers.

"Churches are supposed to be more like a hospital for the sick, for people who need it—we're supposed to welcome anybody. Look at the Bible—Jesus helped the prostitutes, lepers or anybody— and they weren't dressed up!"
— Chad

4

Issue

"For Better, for Worse . . . or Until I Change My Mind"

It was great to be able to spend a second day in the same city, after AudioA's day off yesterday. The majority of the day was spent at Horizons Studio, because AudioA was scheduled to record a video there. After that, we held our discussion in the studio. The pace was slow, the setting laid-back and we were able to relax. Jim prayed with us.

Then he opened the talk by saying, "The biggest problem in America is the disintegration of the family."

Thursday, March 13, 1997

2:32 a.m. Everyone asleep

11:30 a.m. Checked out of motel and headed to venue for lunch—Battelle Hall in Columbus, OH

2:17 p.m. AudioA's video shoot at Horizons Film and Video

3:41 p.m. Issue #4 in the sound studio at Horizons

6:00 p.m. Supper at venue

7:30 p.m. Concert

10:45 p.m. We all helped the sound and lighting crew load out

11:57 p.m. Issue #5 on the bus

"So, why are families falling apart?" Jim asked.

"I think it's because of the absence of God. He is the key factor in keeping relationships together. When I get married, Jesus is going to be first in my wife's life and in mine. My wife will belong to Jesus, not to me. God is giving my wife to me as a gift, because she really belongs to him. I want a wife who has a heart for God. Both of our eyes will be focused on Jesus and then he will be able to work in us. Hopefully, my marriage will be fun and we'll just love each other to death," explained Chad.

"I think a lot of people lose focus on the blessing of having a family. My parents are still together and I'm really blessed to have them, but my dad is not a Christian. I wasn't brought up looking at my dad as this mighty man of God. Seeing God as my Abba Father has been a process. It's very different than my earthly father," Lisa responded. "I think when you look at the divorce rate, we've lost our values. Years ago, there was more of a godly focus within families. Divorce wasn't an option as a way out of the marriage. People today say, 'If it doesn't work out, I can always get out of the relationship.'"

The emotion of being in love definitely fades away—it comes and goes. There are times I want to go see a movie by myself, but there are other times when there is no way I could live without my wife. - Mark

It sounds good and everything, but right now, I can say I'm not going to get divorced. - Rachel

The Bible says you should divorce only because of [someone's] unfaithfulness. I think it would be so hard to know that my wife had cheated on me. I don't know if I could forgive her. - David

There's this story in the Bible about the prophet Hosea, who was told to go and marry an unfaithful wife. What if God calls us to take someone like that back? - Will

When asked why sex and faithfulness is such a big deal in marriage, Chad responded, "Isn't it a spiritual bonding process? You become one with another person."

"When it comes to someone cheating on you, I would hope that I would forgive her and continue to love her. God is ultimately calling us to always forgive. But what if she did it again? That would be a life of torture—having an unfaithful spouse would be a hard thing to go through," Mark said.

Jim asked, "What if your husband doesn't cheat, but he ignores you? He treats people at work better than he treats you, he embarrasses you or he just doesn't meet any of your needs. How would you hang in there?"

"I wouldn't," Vicki reacted.

"But you promised him you would—at the altar. You said, 'For better or worse, in good times and bad, for richer for poorer. I will stay with you and the only thing that will separate us is death.' You promised that," added Jim.

"Well, you'd already be living in a dead marriage. I don't know. Walking out probably wouldn't be the best thing to do. However, if I were ever in that situation, it would be easy to feed on my emotions and say, 'I don't want to be in it,'" responded Vicki.

I would hope that if I am ever in that situation, I would cling, and cling, to God to carry me through that time, and I would put my security in him. My dependence should be on God, rather than on my husband. Hopefully, through a lot of prayer and commitment, his heart might be changed where we could come to a middle ground in our marriage. My parents went through somewhat of a process like that. I can't even fathom my husband coming up to me and saying, "I don't love you anymore." — Lisa

I think you should count on that before going into it. You have to decide at times, "I choose to be in this relationship." There comes a point when you decide, "We're a family now." My wife feels like that sometimes, because I'm gone 80 percent of the year. Even in a marriage, you can count on moments of loneliness. At other times, it all pays off, because you have someone to share with on this level of commitment.

When it comes down to it, there is one person who will be with you forever. I've got Will and Bob and I've known these guys for a long time, but even when these guys are gone, or other friends in my life come and go, there's no security there— but my wife is going to be mine forever. - Mark

If you were to look in the dictionary and write a definition for love, how would you define the love that has to be in place for a marriage to work? — Jim

It means making a choice with someone. It is a commitment in which you die to self and are giving to this person. Ultimately, you become a part of making this person all he is meant to be for God and you help him conform to the image of Christ. It's unconditional love—no matter what. . . . My parents are divorced, but the word "divorce" is not gonna be in my vocabulary.

If [my future husband] wants to leave, I'm not going to chain him to me but, if he doesn't hold up to his end of the bargain doesn't mean that I'm not going to. God has given us free will. Marriage is a choice. . . . I think [I'll marry] someone who has a heart for full-time ministry. I'm into the fairy-tale thing. - Scotia

I believe it is a commitment through thick and thin. You remain committed to that person no matter what. It means being selfless and giving to your marriage, even when you want to walk away. - Lisa

I would like to have my kids talk to me. I hope that they would be comfortable with me and be who they are when they're around me. If my kid makes a bad decision, I would rather know about it. - John

I've always wanted to be the best dad. I also want to be the best grandpa. - Will

My dad was always the one laying down the law. I think it will be harder to be a friend to my kids than to be tough. - Mark

What kind of parent are you going to be?
— Jim

I want to be the kind of parent who instills godly values in my kids. It is important to me to have a personal involvement in their lives. I want my kids to have a clear picture of biblical values and search out God for themselves. I want my kids to do that early. I think you can be a mother and a best friend. I want that kind of respectful relationship. - Scotia

It scares me to death. I don't have the answers and I don't know how I would handle my kids. I can say the way I would like things to be, but I just don't know. - Vicki

100

What can a student do to iron things out with a mom or dad who he's not been getting along with? — Jim

I had to come to a point where I realized I wanted a relationship with my dad. It was important enough that I started to step out and pursue him. I was 14 or 15 years old when I started to do that. I knew that my respect for him would make a difference. It was hard to have a conversation with him, because it was very foreign to me. I would say, "Don't want for your parent to take the first step. If you do, you will miss out." — Lisa

Some relationships are not worth mending. - John

I don't agree with that, because it's not biblical. God is perfect and he doesn't have that attitude with us. As imperfect people, we shouldn't have that kind of attitude either. Growing up means getting out of your comfort zone, even when you'd rather go in your room. Relationships are not about being selfish. My relationship with my father is still difficult. I didn't speak to him for over three years. He would come to my dance concerts, and I would just walk out another door. I've lived in 15 different houses. My dad was living in some really nice places and my mom and I were living in dumps. He wasn't really a father to me. However, since that time, God has really convicted me about reaching out to him. It's hard but that's what God's calling me to do. That's when the kid side of me started dying and I started becoming an adult. My father is worth it, not because he's worth something to me, but because he's worth something to God. God said, 'It's a healing process I want to take you through.'
Now, I see him once a month. It's gonna take years to get to the place where God wants us to be, although we'll probably never perfectly get there. God never said it would be easy. If I reconcile and strengthen my relationship with my father, then it should be a red flag for others. I think relationships spill over. I think a lot has spilled over to my relationship with God. If I deal with my relationship with my father, it will help my relationship with God. - Scotia

If you work on relationships, sometimes it's up to the other person to respond. - Lisa

You may want your dad to say to you, "Hey, I want to be that person," but he never does. - Vicki

It's an illusion, sometimes it's not in your control. - Rachel

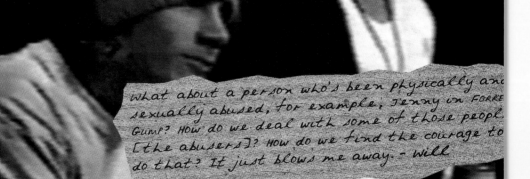

What about a person who's been physically and sexually abused, for example, Jenny in FORREST GUMP? HOW do we deal with some of those people [the abusers]? HOW do we find the courage to do that? It just blows me away. - Will

There are situations in our lives where God gives us the strength. The only way to deal with it is for God to stand beside you. - Lisa

What do you think, Vicki? - Scotia

It's just like a hole that is so raw. I don't think it can ever be mended. When people say God is your Father, I think, "No, he's not a dad." I want an earthly father. I don't have that kind of relationship and I don't think I'll ever have one. - Vicki

The situation I'm going through now is so weird. My dad left when I was two years old. For some reason, maybe it's the kind of person I am or the role model of my grandpa, or other relatives, but I never held that against him. I forgave him and I still loved him. But my twin sister held a grudge most of her life. Now that she's becoming a Christian, she's starting to work through that part of her life. Recently, she's come to a point where she's dealing with it, but it's hard to do that. - Will

My dad's the type that we will all sit around the pool and drink beers. We're a nonemotional family. It's not like, "Oh, I love you." My dad is cool to hang out with. I'm sure at some point I should express the way I feel. It feels like someone is physically holding me back from what I want. I've never really expressed how I feel to my dad. He can't do anything about it now. We can't go back through all those years. - Vicki

I CAN'T RELATE TO HAVING A BROKEN FAMILY AT ALL. I HAVE A PERFECT FAMILY. WE HAVE OUR LITTLE PROBLEMS, BUT IT'S NOTHING MAJOR . . . MY FAMILY IS LIKE "LEAVE IT TO BEAVER." — CHAD

The guys in the band make fun of me and call me Richie Cunningham. . . . Have you ever seen "HAPPY DAYS"? My family is just like that. I can't relate to not having a relationship with my father. - Mark

I don't want anyone to feel bad for me; it's just a part of life. - Vicki

I think God brings you to a point of healing or mending. There is something really powerful in that. I've seen that in my heart and in my life. You have to get to know this person. I have great peace in my heart from getting to know my dad better, or in telling him I love him. I just recently went home to see my dad. I had mixed emotions; in some ways, I didn't want to go. In my case, my dad has a life-threatening illness, so it has a way of waking people up. - Will

Families I baby-sit for are all great families not divorced, with a great mom, and a great dad. I feel like God has blessed me and given them to me as examples of how a family should be and what a marriage should be like. - Vicki

I want to be the best husband, but I know I fall short of that; that's when you have to rely on God to work through your marriage. When I was in college, I used to say, "I'm going to make the perfect husband for some woman." I wonder if the same thing will happen when you have children. You say, "I'm going to be the best dad," but when you're in the situation, you have to live it out and you make mistakes along the way— it's a part of life. You have to depend on God to help you do it. - Mark

104

What about sibling rivalry?
— Jim

Sometimes I feel like I have to live up to certain expectations. When you have older siblings, you sense that your parents are waiting to see what you're going to do with your life. They may hope you will be successful like your brother. I don't want to be like my brother, or my sister—I want to be the best I can be. It's not like I don't know what I want to do with my life, I just want to be my own person. I feel like I have to live up to both of them. You have to fit your own frame. - John

Does that make you not want to try at all? In that situation, I see a lot of pressure and some people settle for mediocrity they say, "If I can't have this or achieve a certain success, OK, whatever." I wonder if you've ever felt that? - Will

No, because I know what I want to do with my life. I've never felt that—not at all. But, you do sense a certain pressure from your parents to meet certain expectations. - John

I think there's always sibling rivalry going on. Or you've heard of situations when siblings feel like their parents love another kid more. I would hope that wouldn't happen or that someone's parents wouldn't think like that. - Mark

V

icki changed the focus of the discussion when she said, "I want to know why Rachel was crying."

"I don't want today to be my testimony. I was crying because through the whole conversation, God was trying to tell me that this was my day. I said earlier that my parents almost got divorced. That wasn't the first time and it wasn't the last. It almost happened when I was in seventh grade. Right now it's happening. We all live in the same house—my dad, mom, my sister and me, but it's more like two families. It's not like a family should be. Scotia said she was never going to get a divorce. I said that also, but I wonder how that would change if you had kids," mused Rachel.

"I think the priority relationship is the husband and wife, then the kids are after that. I wouldn't leave because of that, unless I was being abused or if my kids were being abused. I would hope that would shock my husband enough, and he would respond and seek counseling. Hopefully, we would be able to work through the situation. I have seen too many families who have been able to work through a number of circumstances. I know things can be worked out and divorce doesn't have to happen," Scotia observed. Then she asked Rachel, "What about you?"

I've heard my parents yelling at each other. I just wanted it to be over. I didn't want to live like that anymore. I want more than anything for my parents to work things out. I know God can work through the situation, but I don't see change taking place. - Rachel

I used to cry every night. I don't drink, cuss, sleep around; I haven't done anything that people typically do to deal with things; I don't overeat. I don't know how most people would be affected. I don't think I've become numb, but I don't know. It's really hard. Sometimes I feel like I have to be the mediator when it comes to communication. - Rachel

You said that things won't change, so do you want your parents to get a divorce? - Vicki

I don't know what I want. . . . I've prayed every night from fifth grade until I graduated from high school that my parents wouldn't fight. Then, when I graduated from high school, we hit this. I said, "OK, they're not fighting, but they stopped talking." I pray that God's will be done. - Rachel

I have a dad, but he's not really involved in my life. It's sometimes harder when your parents are together and they don't have a relationship, as opposed to when one is here and one is there. Sometimes I wish my dad lived with me. It's harder to know he is involved in my life, but he's really not—I don't know how to balance that. It's either do it, or be done with it—either call me every day, Dad, or don't call me at all. It's OK to feel angry and it's OK to feel pain.
-Vicki

I am feeling pain. I love my parents very much . . . . it's so hard to forgive. - Rachel

What does God think
about marriage and divorce?

"The LORD God said, 'It is not good for the man to be alone. I will make a helper suitable for him.'" Genesis 2:18 NIV "But Jesus said, 'Not everyone is mature enough to live a married life. It requires a certain aptitude and grace. Marriage isn't for everyone. Some, from birth seemingly, never give marriage a thought. Others never get asked—or accepted. And some decide not to get married for kingdom reasons. But if you're capable of growing into the largeness of marriage, do it.'" Matthew 19:11, 12 THE MESSAGE "Be devoted to one another in brotherly love. Honor one another above yourselves. . . . Live in harmony with one another." Romans 12:10, 16 NIV "Submit to one another out of reverence for Christ. . . . Each one of you also must love his wife as he loves himself, and the wife must respect her husband." Ephesians 5:21, 33 NIV

Although only one in 10 married people think there is a possibility of divorce in their future, statistics indicate that nearly twice that many adults actually wind up in divorce court, leaving 27% of all children with only one parent at home.

"I don't want anyone to feel bad for me; it's just a part of life. . . . It's OK to feel angry and it's OK to feel pain." — Vicki

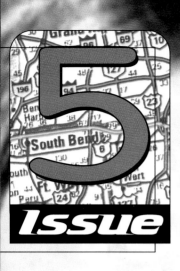

5

Issue

"Please Notice Me"

...pics like piercing and ta...
things people do to get noticed. We addresse...
reasons why they do it.

Friday, March 14, 1997

12:11 a.m. Wheels roll to the Windy City

12:20 a.m. Issue #5 on the road

1:55 a.m. Stopped at Pilot Travel Center and Dairy Queen in Eaton, Ohio

2:25 a.m. Some go to sleep, others watch PATRIOT GAMES

4:15 a.m. All asleep

11:00 a.m. Woke up and showered in Chicago

12:00 p.m. Lunch at the Rosemont Horizon with Marty and Ovey

"**A**fter 13 years of youth ministry, I don't understand why people are sticking things in their bodies. I don't get it. Why do people pierce their tongues or other parts of their bodies?" Jim began.

John: "What don't you like about it? Why don't you like it—does it scare you?"

Jim: "No, it doesn't scare me—I just don't understand it. I think it's ridiculous that people would stick something through their body parts."

Chad: "It's just fashion."

Jim: "Why would you stick something through your body—like your tongue or whatever?"

Lisa: "Well, I had my belly button pierced three years ago. Why did I get it pierced? It was just something I wanted to do."

Will: "Is it still pierced?"

Lisa: "Yes."

Jim: "Why did you want to do it?"

Lisa: "I was living in Hawaii at the time. It was one of those moments, where my roommate and I decided we wanted to do something different, so we got our belly buttons pierced."

You were so bored that you had to stick something through your body? — Jim

> No, it wasn't because I was bored. I wanted to do it. I don't mind having my belly button pierced. I like that. Why do people get two holes pierced in their ears? - Lisa

Ears are traditional. — Jim

> Ears weren't traditional 10 years ago. Everybody was freaking out about that too. - John

> All of the girls who are here have their ears pierced. It's customary. Body piercing—it's the same thing. . . . Why is it such big deal? I'm not catching it. — Chad

I think a safety pin through someone's eyebrow is screaming out for more than a fashion statement. — Jim

> Do you think they are screaming out for attention? - John

I think they are screaming out for more than attention. — Jim

> You can't generalize that. Some individuals do it for that reason, but I think some people wear polos to get attention too. I think it's a rebellious fashion statement today. A lot of people are doing it. — Chad

112

So, it's rebellion? — Jim

NO, IN THE '80s, IT WAS THE SPIKED, COLORED HAIR, AND SEQUINED CLOTHES; IN THE '60s IT WAS THE BELL-BOTTOMS. REBELLIOUS FASHION WAS SOMETHING DIFFERENT THAN THE NORM. — CHAD

I think it's self-expression—people try to express themselves in creative ways. I have a couple of tattoos. I guess it was to do something different, too. Everyone is trying to find his or her little niche. Whether it is fashion, or whatever—some people choose to combine polyester with T-shirts to create their own look. It's like, "This is my look, this is what I like." - Will

People did things to alter their appearance 20 years ago to receive attention, like wearing different clothes. Now people have tattoos or are into body piercing. There's nothing else to wear, so they try doing things to their body. It's just style—20 years from now we won't think anything about it - Bob

I want to put this together. I'm not slammin' it. I am trying to understand. If someone is screaming out for attention, there are so many other ways. Mother Teresa stands out because she's so good and wants to help so many people. In the '60s, people who wanted to be radical, including Christians, marched for causes. They didn't pierce things. A white Christian who wanted to be radical marched with Martin Luther King, Jr. That was more radical than putting a sword through your tongue. Those people made a statement. What difference, what statement does piercing something make for Christ? — Jim

"Singers or people

that are leaders for Christ reach out to different types of people. When it comes to music, you may see a group all wearing ties, or some with earrings who have dyed their hair. You'll find that people are interested in them partially because of their appearance. It's a way to blend in. People respond when they see someone who looks like they do. They say, 'Wait a minute, they are like me—I wonder what they're about.' If you see somebody who is like you, you want to know what that person is about. It makes them curious, so they want to listen," David explained.

"I agree with that," Will said.

"So many people are buying into it. With everybody piercing their ears to make a rebellious statement, their alternative isn't alternative anymore—it's mainstream," Jim remarked. "If you are going to stand out and make your positive statement on the world, I think it would be by living out your faith. Living out your faith—I believe that's an alternative lifestyle."

We used to challenge kids and tell them that if they wanted to be a rebel, then they should be like Jesus, because to be like Jesus is totally against the norm today. - Will

So, tell me why somebody would stick a sword through his tongue? — Jim

I haven't had anything pierced, but I can see a Christian doing it to relate to other people. It might be a way to win them to Christ. - David

The body is the temple of God and we're not supposed to smoke or drink excessive amounts of alcohol because (those habits) destroy our body. Do you agree with that? Do you think hanging gaudy things off your body honors it? — Jim

The things you hang off of it aren't gaudy. Like I said before, I think if you do it excessively, there could be a problem. - David

DRINKING CAFFEINE OR EATING FAST FOOD CAN BE HARMFUL TO YOUR BODY—AND YOUR BODY IS A TEMPLE. BUT WE ALL DO IT—IT'S THE SAME THING. — CHAD

You're saying we are all going to do bad stuff, so it's OK to go ahead and do bad things? — Jim

No, we are saying we don't think body piercing is destroying your body. What does it do to harm your body? - David

How does it honor your body? — Jim

In some people's eyes, it makes the body more beautiful. - John

I think a good example of this is the Christian music industry. It has changed so much over the past few years. Christianity now is not just singing hymns or real soft music. I realize you don't have to be this certain type of Christian. You can be anything you want; you can wear whatever clothes you want. You can be your own person. - David

I WOULDN'T LISTEN TO AUDIOA OR ALL THESE OTHER BANDS IF I PICKED THEM UP AND THEY HAD A BORING COVER WITH A '40S LOOK TO IT, IF THEY WERE WEARING SUITS AND TIES, IF THEY STOOD AROUND AND PLAYED GUITAR. THE WAY A GROUP DRESSES CATCHES MY EYE. — CHAD

They can reach out to a whole new group of people for Christ—those who have never been touched before—primarily because of the way they are dressed. - David

Do you ever reach a place when you say, "This is too far."?

— Jim

IF YOU'RE SINNING OR IF YOU'RE NOT GLORIFYING GOD. — CHAD

If all you are is of God, then decorating, piercing and tattooing is in line with the rest of your lifestyle—I don't see a problem with it. I don't understand it because I don't personally have a desire, but I won't condemn someone else who does. - Scotia

You were never called to be "your own person," you were called to be Christ's person. — Jim

I think [you should] be who you are, as yourself, and not to fit in with other people. - David

Do you see any pattern in Jesus' life where he did that? — Jim

Yeah, he didn't hang out with all the high-class people to be high class. - David

What did he do to be like those people? — Jim

He hung out with all the people that were low. - David

HE BECAME ALL THINGS TO ALL PEOPLE. — CHAD

I think Will can minister to people by looking like this. - David

What about a straight-edge ministry, though? David and Chad were talking about how you can reach different people, who you can relate to. Can you go into a club? - Will

Do you really think that most people are doing this for outreach? Do they say, "OK, I'm going to build a bridge of friendship with somebody"? — Jim

No, but I do think there are a group of people who do it for those reasons. - David

I PERSONALLY JUST THINK [TONGUE PIERCING] IS REALLY COOL. MY PARENTS DON'T WANT ME TO DO IT, NOR DO MY FRIENDS, BUT I WANT TO. — CHAD

Just because they don't want you to do it, does that make it wrong? - David

If he decides to do it, does that make him sinful? . . . My parent's won't let me. They won't support college or anything if I get a tattoo or have something pierced. ↳ John

Jim if your kids come to you when they get older and want to get their tongues pierced, what would you say to them? - John

I would ask them not to. However, if they are adults, they can do what they want, but I would ask them not to. — Jim

But what if they do? - John

I'd still love them. — Jim

Are you going to punish them? - John

How am I going to punish a 20 year old? — Jim

What if they are in high school? - David

If they expect me to pay the bills, I would tell them no. — Jim

What about when your dad said, "If you get an earring, I won't pay for college"? - David

I think he had the right to do that, though I didn't like it. — Jim

Did you think it was wrong then, or do you think it's wrong now? - David

It ticked me off then. At that time I probably thought he was wrong. But, I also thought it was wrong that he wanted me in by 10 p.m. (Actually, I never had a curfew.) I think honoring your parents is the choice. If your parents ask you to do certain things, there is generally a good reason for it. — Jim

"I think we need to challenge

the older generation. I've never thought about body piercing, but I did want another hole in my ear. My mother didn't want me to. I was disobedient, so this would not be an example to follow. I thought that if she wouldn't take me to get my ear pierced I would do it myself. I numbed my ear with ice, got a needle and pierced another hole in it. When my mother came home and saw it, she said, 'Are you crazy? You could have caught an infection, or anything could have happened.' So, then she took me to get it professionally done and she got over it.

"I think there are definite areas where you should obey your parents, but there are some areas where we can challenge them. We should be able to establish our own identity," Scotia observed.

"When I got it done the first time, my mom thought I had gone to a dirty place and got AIDS. I would like parents to be open to go with their kids, so they can see what it's like. . . . I saw a lot of signs when I was in L.A. On every bench and bus stop: piercing, tattooing, [signs like] 'If you have AIDS, call this telephone number,'" Scotia continued.

"Well, in the area where you were, people were giving out tattoos with guitar strings," John remarked.

Chad told a recent story concerning the perceptions of people in his church toward him: "When I had my hair dyed fire-engine red a few months ago, I stuck out and I was freaky looking. There was a lady who attended our church. She said that she had problems being accepted at other churches. But, at our church, she said she saw people who were different that were accepted, so she felt welcome. In the past, she thought Christian churches didn't accept people who were different. Later, she told my parents that the only reason she decided to stay was because she felt that if the minister's son looked different, yet was still accepted, she would also be accepted there. Recently she became a Christian. My parents took back all their comments about my hair. As an end result, they felt something good came out of it."

Do you think the church has come to a point of accepting this? - David

I think there are pockets of the church that have. — Jim

Basically, we are the church. How should we respond to these people? What are we called to do? We talk about unwed mothers and how having sex before marriage is wrong. A girl doesn't have an abortion, because an abortion is wrong. We let [a person like this] in our church. Are we accepting different people because of what they do, even though they sin? When they mess up, do we let them into the church? I don't see that happening. I don't see the church saying to the freak, "You're welcome, you are loved here." Yet, we say we should love those people. I don't see the homosexual walking into a church saying, "I am dealing with this—I don't know if it's right or wrong. Can you love me, help me and tell me if it is right or wrong?" - Will

The church has to do that—we are called to respond to those people. I taught a lesson once on homosexuality. After the lesson, one guy came up to me and said, "I disagree with what you said." I responded, "That's OK, I really respect you for staying." Another time, a guy came up to me and told me he was a homosexual. I hugged him. He wasn't expecting that from me. Sometimes you have to pray for God to give you wisdom in different situations. . . .

On Wednesday nights, my youth group looks like a night club. I have 50 kids smoking in the parking lot. I have Christian parents who drive their kids around the parking lot and don't let them out around the ones who are smoking, because they don't like the kids I attract. It's not about someone's kid already being saved. I want my saved kids to have a passion for those people who don't know the Lord yet, and they need a place to bring them. It's not to shove Jesus down their throats. I want them to go to McDonald's afterwards and discuss the issues that came up in that setting. I have one rule in my youth group and that's to show respect for other people.
— Jim

That brings up an interesting point with our ministry. If God ever called us to do shows in a secular venue or tour with a non-Christian band, would we go into clubs? The way we would approach it is to call up youth ministers and tell them ahead of time that we are going on this secular tour and we would love for them to show up and support us in this environment. In the back of our minds, we'd be scared to death asking, "Are they going to think we went secular-or that we're not Christians anymore?" Some people bash Christian artists like Amy Grant or dc Talk because they've come to a level in which they are successful in both secular and Christian environments. - Will

My attitude is the sooner that you get there, the better. We'll send you there. You are missionaries to the world. — Jim

If you play for a Christian crowd, you're basically preaching to the [Saved]. The primary opportunities you would have to win people to Christ would be if someone brought their non-Christian friends. People need to understand their motivation. — Scotia

What does everyone think about Jars of Clay? — Will

I THINK WHAT THEY'VE DONE TO THIS POINT IS AWESOME. GOD IS USING THEM TREMENDOUSLY. — CHAD

They don't compromise their stance or their faith. They need to open up for Pearl Jam; they need to be out there. — Jim

"I get bored, I need change, but the one thing I don't like is when you look at other people and make judgments about them. That ticks me off. I think you should accept people the way they are. Some people say, 'I'm not going to talk to them because they are pierced, or because there is something different about their appearance.' It should be all about your heart. Each individual is a person," Vicki stressed.

"I don't know if the world will ever come to a point where everybody will accept everyone, to realize that the true character of a person is who they are on the inside," David agreed.

"The sooner the church realizes that it exists for the world and not for itself, the better. Your youth group is not about already being saved. Everything has already been done, because Jesus died on the cross. It's only working on a few details after that. After you're saved, the only thing you have left to do is to bring someone else in," Jim preached.

Some people do different things because they truly want attention and they need help; some people do it for artsy reasons; some people do it because it feels good. What do we do with those people? They aren't necessarily doing it to be good; maybe they are trying to seek attention in the wrong way, or the only way that they can. If we do what they do, to some of them it may be considered a stumbling block. . . . We minister to people who have piercing. What do we do when we win them to Christ? Do they take the piercing out? – Scotia

Everyone has different ways of getting attention and becoming accepted. What classifies body piercing as wrong? – David

I think we are all the same. Some people get pierced, others may go to the gym six days a week and blow their body up, or they might get a perm twice a week and have their nails done. Everyone is screaming out, "Somebody like me!" . . . I don't see it as right or wrong. From my perspective as a youth pastor, I see body piercing as people trying to express who they are. My job is to respond, to look beyond the color of their hair, the size of their muscle or how much money is inside their wallet and say, "I want to see your heart." — Jim

I think the bottom line is that everyone seeks love and acceptance. Whether it is piercing or whatever, that is a way of getting it. People who have low self-esteem will do various things to get attention. Some girls wear provocative clothing because it makes them feel better about themselves. I think homosexuality and bisexuality can be a cry for attention. It's the artsy thing to do. Some people do it for the shock value. I think what they are really looking for is to be loved for who they are. – Will

Issue #5

What does God think
about who we are?

"What is man that you are mindful of him, the son of man that you care for him? You made him a little lower than the heavenly beings and crowned him with glory and honor." Psalm 8:4, 5 NIV "For you created my inmost being; you knit me together in my mother's womb. I praise you because I am fearfully and wonderfully made." Psalm 139:13, 14 NIV "But by the grace of God I am what I am, and his grace to me was not without effect. No, I worked harder than all of them—yet not I, but the grace of God that was with me." 1 Corinthians 15:10 NIV

"I don't know if we will ever come to a point where everybody will accept everyone, to realize that the true character of a person is who they are on the inside."
— David

Issue 6

▶

0:06:30:15
57min

"Facing Our Prejudice"

We rolled out of our bunks and headed to

the Rosemont Horizon for showers. Our agenda for the day included a trip to inner-city Chicago where we were going to embark on a fact-finding mission of the homeless. We set out to discover what the church can do to reach out to these people. At lunch we met two very interesting guys, Marty and Ovey. Ovey is one of 50,000 Romanians who live in Chicago. They told us some stories about people they have seen living on the streets and some of the harsh realities of that kind of existence. They also talked about the inner-city Chicago ministry that they are involved in, and how they are committed to ministering to the homeless people there. They admitted that it is challenging at times. However, they are optimistic and feel God is working in these people's lives.

After we ate, we loaded up in vans and drove through downtown Chicago. Marty and Ovey were very friendly and shared with us a lot of stories about their lives and backgrounds. They talked a lot about history and their culture.

Friday, March 14, 1997

2:12 p.m. Drove through downtown Chicago

2:55 p.m. Under the bridge

3:51 p.m. One van heads back to venue for AudioA's sound check; the other van heads to the el station (overhead railway)

5:00 p.m. Sound check

6:30 p.m. First-class catering, while we watch round one coverage of the NCAA basketball tournament

7:30 p.m. Carolyn Arends' set

7:55 p.m. AudioA comes out to a screaming audience wearing glow-in-the-dark necklaces

9:30 p.m. Opening night of RETURN OF THE JEDI

Saturday, March 15, 1997

12:30 p.m. In-store event at John's Bookshop in Wheaton, IL, where SCC, AudioA and Carolyn Arends sign autographs

1:10 p.m. Issue #6

2:05 p.m. We close the place up

0:38:50: 24min

0:49:45:1 12m

We saw the tallest building, Sears Tower, and other sights downtown. Then we arrived at a bridge on Lower Wacker St. and drove under it. We parked the vans, got out and met some of those who were living under the bridge. All their beds and belongings were lined up in a row. Many of them were sitting around, solemn and quiet. Others were socializing with their friends. The people there were slow to warm up to us, especially at first—and understandably so, because we had invaded their home.

We brought some chicken and a case of Pepsi to hand out to them. Both were gone in a matter of minutes. Our group divided up and we began talking to the homeless people. Some were friendly, others kept their distance and a few of them didn't want anything to do with us. We noticed that the people could keep warm there, because of the heater from the subway blowing on them. The place smelled like urine, and even when we got back into the vans, we could smell it. Marty said it was because it was on our shoes.

We sang "Amazing Grace" with them, along with a few choruses before we left. Then we said good-bye as we got back into the vans. Everyone had mixed emotions. Some of us were quiet on the way back through town. As we were leaving, Scotia had tears running down her face, but remained silent. We knew she was upset about something. Marty and Ovey shared some more about their Romanian church and their outreach to these homeless people. There are about 20 people involved in their ministry "under the bridge." They have a gospel choir and they often go downtown and sing. Ovey said, "We take them sandwiches, coffee, hot cocoa or pop. We are not yet to the stage to take them the gospel, but we want to get there. We have to establish a friendship with them first."

Tonight AudioA

performed to a packed-out crowd at the Rosemont. John had been talking about the opening of RETURN OF THE JEDI all week. Seventeen of us left the venue after AudioA's set and traveled to a near-by theater. The movie ran over two hours and we got out about 11:45 p.m. (We were supposed to be at a bookstore for autographs at midnight and the theater was about a half an hour away.) Bob was the only AudioA member who didn't go to the movie. All the way back from the movie, Mark kept saying that they were going to get in big trouble.

We arrived back at the venue to pick up a few more people, then rushed over to the book-store in Wheaton. People were waiting around for the rest of the band to arrive. When we finally did, Steven Curtis Chapman jokingly muttered, "Audio Delinquent." We walked around the store while AudioA signed autographs. Then, we sat down in the music area of the store and launched into issue #6.

Norridge Theatre

Tonight we saw RETURN OF THE JEDI." We are all very thankful and proud that we were part of saving John's life. He will not have to die now because he has seen all three of the new STAR WARS films on the day that they were released. - Rachel

127

Issue #6

I want to go home.

Today, we went to a place where there are people living under a bridge in Chicago. I talked to a man named Jerry who is going home to his family next week, after two years of living on and off the street. He is a Christian and he's looking forward to starting a new job on the same week that he moves home.

Having worked with homeless people on several occasions, I have come to believe that you can't make generalizations. A lot of people say that they [the homeless] are lazy and they need to get a job just so they can sleep easier at night and not feel bad about not being part of a solution.

The most ignorant things that I heard said today came from the people that I was there with. I heard things like, "I can't have much sympathy for people who can work," "I feel like I'm in a zoo" (as we drove through Cabrini Green housing projects), or "We should be safe since we have an African-American with us." (As if I am an interpreter or some kind of shield.) I could feel absolute hatred rising in me. I wanted to say something, but I knew I would curse, scream and cry so I held back until I could get myself together.

I hate seeing black people, my people, in that state. Poverty and homelessness should stir compassion in Christians. Any Joe-on-the-street can say, "Go get a job" and then forget about it it surprised me that brothers and sisters in Christ could [say such things]. – Scotia

00:08.51.09

PLAY   LOCK

128

"I was moved today because some comments were made that were very offensive to me. I was angry and I was hurt," Scotia began.

Jim asked, "Like what?"

"We were driving through Cabrini Green and one person said, 'I feel like I'm in a zoo or something.' That was offensive to me because the people they were [referring to] were just like me," explained Scotia.

"Do you think they were talking about being black or white? Meaning, 'Look at all the black people in the zoo'?" Jim inquired. He went on to explain that this wasn't the case when the comment was made.

"Regardless, they were just like me, and it was offensive," Scotia said. "There were two black men walking behind the van when we drove up. Someone said, 'Hey look, two real gang members.' It was just two black men walking down the street. If two white men were walking down the street, we wouldn't say, 'Hey look, there's two doctors, lawyers or construction workers.' But two gang members? If you were

in a car with all black people, and we went through a white neighborhood and I said, 'Hey look, there are two Klansmen walking down the street,' that would be offensive to you. Even if it isn't offensive to you, it was offensive to me."

Scotia continued,

"Other comments were made like: 'They just need to get a job,' or 'I don't understand because they can get jobs.' John said, 'You can't generalize—you have to take it case by case.' I thought, that's the first smart thing that I've heard all day. We can't generalize because I don't think the majority of those people would choose to live in their urine, in the cold. A lot of them have mental illnesses; some of them are paralyzed. I have been a paycheck away from being homeless. There have been situations where if I didn't have family to live with, or my mother and brother didn't have other people that they could live with—we would have been in a shelter. When you live like that, if someone gets sick and can't work for a month, they don't get paid—then you're out. There's just no way to catch up, no overtime, no money, no place to borrow. There's nothing you can do but not pay your bills and get kicked out.

"I don't think a lot of people who say, 'They just need to go get a job' really understand that if someone misses two weeks of work, then they can be out on the street because they don't have family or a place to go. We did—I am thankful to God that we did. If we didn't, I would have been in a homeless shelter."

"Those men that we saw on the street—they sit there 24 hours a day," interjected Jim.

"I'm not saying all of them don't choose that," Scotia agreed.

"Case by case," John echoed.

"**A** lot of people sit back and say, 'They can get jobs.' They sleep comfortably in their beds at night, in their nice homes, without really believing that there are people living like that. But, they're not being part of the solution. They sit back and say, 'If they really wanted to make it, they could make it.' They choose to live like that and they roll over in their nice warm beds.

"Today, I experienced seeing other black people look at me like I was a traitor for walking around with you. One guy ran into me in the subway and said, 'Fine, don't move, b***h,' and ran into me. I felt alienated from other black people because I was with you and I also felt disrespected by you, the people that I was with," Scotia said. "I felt alone and I wanted to go home. It was disappointing and it really hurt me that it was my brothers and sisters in Christ."

"I can tell you why I made that comment," Jim explained. "I felt totally out of place, like I was on a tour bus that goes through the zoo. 'On your left, you'll find the homeless and on your right, you'll find Cabrini Green, where people shoot at you.' My statement was almost a parody on that. I felt really out of place by going and staring at homeless people. I don't think we did anybody a big favor. I felt like we were on a tour of the outcasts of society. I wasn't making a statement about the people that lived there, I was making a statement about how I felt being there."

"I didn't take it that way. Vicki shared some other comments with me. I wanted to go. I threw up a wall. Then Vicki talked with me and challenged me not to do that," said Scotia.

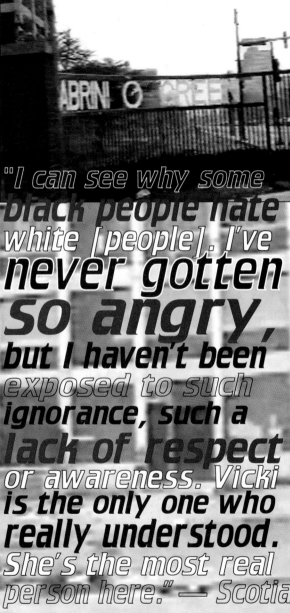

"I can see why some black people hate white [people]. I've never gotten so angry, but I haven't been exposed to such ignorance, such a lack of respect or awareness. Vicki is the only one who really understood. She's the most real person here." — Scotia

there and why we wanted to film them. They wanted us to pay them for filming them. If I was down on my luck and I was living there, I wouldn't want anyone taping me. I talked to one guy who was worried about his mom seeing him like that. - Mark

Vicki and I talked to one guy and he was telling us how he was going to get a job and move on from there. He was really inspirational to me, because I have a lot of material things and I'm always thinking about how bad things are. The guy we talked to expressed a lot of hope-I walked away seeing that. - David

I'm different than most of you here. I'm cynical, but I said, "why are we going here if these people choose to be here?" Why make a big deal over it? I've been through times in my life when it would have been easier not to deal with anything, when it would have been easier to grab a bottle of whiskey and drown my sorrows away. I've been close to that before, but I chose not to react that way. I know those people need some kind of help, but when I think of homeless people, I think of a mother who has a child and can't afford to go pay for her food and they get kicked out of their house. Those people need help.

I probably stick my foot in my mouth and say things that offend people, but that's how I feel. It doesn't matter who they are, or what color they are, I feel that way. I've said this before, "Sometimes I rely on myself too much and I probably should rely on God more." I think you have to work hard and do things and take responsibility for your life. Maybe I'm wrong on that to a certain degree. I know we all have to rely on God, but I don't think we should use that as an excuse to do things that seem easy at the time. - Bob

I have lived paycheck to paycheck. I've missed meal because we couldn't afford it.
— Scotia

THE THING THAT HIT ME ON OUR LITTLE TRIP DOWNTOWN WASN'T SO MUCH THE SITUATION. BUT THE THOUGHT CROSSED MY MIND, "WHAT IF GOD CALLED ME TO MINISTER TO THOSE PEOPLE?" (JIM AND I TALKED ABOUT THIS YESTERDAY.) WHAT IF HE CALLED ME TO MINISTER TO HOMELESS PEOPLE WHERE I LIVE, OR IN CHICAGO OR WHEREVER? WOULD I WANT TO IN THE FIRST PLACE? OR WOULD I BE ABLE TO RELATE TO THEM? TRUTHFULLY, WHEN THE QUESTION CROSSED MY MIND, I WAS LIKE, "I DON'T WANT TO. I REALLY DON'T WANT TO GO DOWN AND MINISTER TO HOMELESS PEOPLE. — CHAD

"I was into drugs before I knew the Lord. I thought I knew the street, until I met these guys in the inner city. I had a desire and a heart to do it, but at first I didn't know how to get involved. I was in a Bible study and a friend talked to me about getting involved in this ministry. Now we have a group of people who go down there every week." — Marty

"One day I saw a homeless man begging for money and I got mad. I was working, earning money, and I thought he could work too. Marty talked to me about it. He said, "Be happy. You grew up in a Christian family with values. This guy never knew that nor had someone to show him that kind of love." I realized people need the love of Christ and I decided to become involved in taking the gospel to them." — Ovey

Scotia, I know you are upset. I didn't mean to say anything to hurt your feelings. I know there were people living in that situation that were down on their luck, but I heard several people say that they chose to live there. I said, "Why do you choose to be here?" Even if they were to go to a nasty apartment, it would be a better environment than where they are now. I lived in a nasty apartment for awhile. If I offended anybody, I apologize. I stick my foot in my mouth a lot. - Bob

Apart from Christ, why would people be motivated to go work a job for $2 an hour, if they can smoke their day away? Why should someone be motivated to face reality the harsh reality of the real world-when he can go down there and drink it up with his friends? What purpose is there to life apart from Christ? If we are not taking Christ to people, then keep your chicken. That's not making a difference in those people's lives. They can get food on their own. - Scotia

The first thing that we have to keep in mind is that we can't make a blanket statement about anybody or any group of people. We can't say all white, black, homeless or Spanish people, or all church leaders or elderly people are this or that. You can't say all—we've already established that—but what can we do to help people that are on the street, homeless, or have already passed the point of being one paycheck away from being on the street? What can we do to make a difference in that corner of the world? — Jim

I felt odd being "John-cam" for the day. I felt bad. What am I doing? It was like trying to capture an animal on tape, or something. I heard someone say, "Did you get that shot; are you getting this?" This happens every day and it was invading those people's privacy. - John

A lot of Christians think they can get on an airplane and fly to Haiti or Africa, then they come home and feel like they did a good thing. Yet, they sit in math class with 30 people that are going to Hell and they have no problem sleeping at night. — Jim

I saw an MTV special report once that was supposedly about a cult on a college campus. It turned out to be the FCA (Fellowship of Christian Athletes). The report talked about people coming up to freshmen in college and making friends with them, inviting them to various activities. People responded to it because they were lonely. They were trying to win them over to their religion, which happened to be Christianity. It was considered this big facade. They were forming all these relationships with kids and then just dropping them. They reported it as this big cult. They would bring these kids in, but they weren't really forming relationships with them, because they were always seeking out new people to bring in. From the outside, I can understand why people would question what they were doing. It appeared very hypocritical and ridiculous. . . .

It's almost like putting on a mask. The people we saw today will probably never see me again. They don't even know my name, but when you go and talk to your neighbor, you have to see them every day. I felt like a fool when we said, "Let's sing 'Amazing Grace' underneath this bridge." You are willing to do it because in a half an hour, you'll be gone. It's a different story for those guys who minister there every week. Yet, you wouldn't make a fool for Jesus around people that you see every day, around people who will ridicule you in your math class, or where you work. - Mark

nister to know we
e Christians. I think
is important to form
lationships with
em first. When I
ow each person by
me, then I will feel
at I've come to a
ace to start sharing
e gospel with them."

Ovey

What does God think
about our prejudice?

"If a man enters your church wearing an expensive suit, and a street person wearing rags comes in right after him, and you say to the man in the suit, 'Sit here, sir; this is the best seat in the house!' and either ignore the street person or say, 'Better sit here in the back row,' haven't you segregated God's children and proved that you are judges who can't be trusted? Listen, dear friends. Isn't it clear by now that God operates quite differently? He chose the world's down-and-out as the kingdom's first citizens, with full rights and privileges. This kingdom is promised to anyone who loves God." James 2:2-5 THE MESSAGE "You, then, why do you judge your brother? Or why do you look down on your brother? For we will all stand before God's judgment seat." Romans 14:10 NIV "There will always be poor people in the land. Therefore I command you to be openhanded toward your brothers and toward the poor and needy in your land." Deuteronomy 15:11 NIV

79% of white Americans believe that African-Americans have equal opportunities at getting jobs, while only 46% of the black population agree. Whites and blacks do agree, however, that race relations will always be an issue.

"You can't generalize—you have to take it *case by case.*"
— John

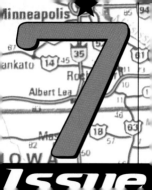

Minneapolis

ankato 14 35 Rochester 61

Albert Lea 18

IOWA

Issue 7

Minneapolis was the coldest

city of the tour. When we arrived, they had several inches of snow on the ground. John didn't bring a coat, so he spent most of the time wearing his sweater over his head to keep warm. Scotia had an extra jacket and someone borrowed it. The Mall of America was huge—there's even an amusement park inside. We were going to hold our discussion inside the mall—as we were walking along, the camera-man noticed a green hot tub and asked permission to use it. We were fully clothed, and there was no water, so most of us sat inside of it. So, the discussion begins . . .

Saturday, March 15, 1997

2:13 a.m. Shopped at Omni Grocery store for snacks; John walked through Taco Bell drive-thru

2:28 a.m. Hit the road for Minneapolis

9:32 a.m. Arrived at the Target Center

11:00 a.m. Showers and lunch where the Timberwolves play

1:27 p.m. Issue #7 in front of Sears, Mall of America

4:48 p.m. Left for venue

5:30 p.m. Mark Stuart had an interview

6:10 p.m. Hair-dying and bleach party

7:10 p.m. Matt Balm (Mr. Merchandise) led devotions

7:50 p.m. AudioA's set

8:25 p.m. We performed "Big House" with them on stage

9:02 p.m. Pizza on the bus and prayer for safe travels and for AudioA's ministry

9:32 p.m. Rolled for Nashville, TN. We arrived by 12:45 p.m. the next day

Jim
you an
and da
going
Shoul
shoul
purpo
Joh
every
Ben:
compan
someone
Vicki:
the pa
in the
Chris
Jim
Vi
j
dat

It is easier for someone to pull you down, than it is for you to pull that person up. You may go into a relationship saying, "I'll date him and bring him to God," but it's not always going to happen. I think it has happened. I think you can build a friendship with somebody. If you allow God to speak through you in that friendship, then you have the opportunity to influence that person for Christ.

For me, I don't say, "I want to date guys who are Christians." I want someone who is on the same level that I am. I don't even say my criteria are to date only Christian guys; I want a Christian, a person who is on my same wavelength. I want someone who is going to challenge me, someone who is going to challenge my relationship with Christ and my love for Christ. I'm looking for someone who will motivate me in stepping forward and growing in that relationship with Christ. It is a big attraction when I can look at a man of God and want to worship and love God even more. - Lisa

I won't date anyone who's not a Christian. Some people have a certain plan or criteria that they establish and they don't change their minds. - Ben

What about witnessing to someone that you're dating? — Jim

It worked for me. We were friends for seven months and I had the opportunity to tell her about the Lord, but I got to the point in our relationship where I was having feelings for her more than just a friend. During that time, we established our friendship; we became closer and learned about each other. We weren't physically involved. I said, "I really can't date you anymore because you're not going to know the love I know. I know God, the creator of love."

It came to the point that she wasn't willing to go the next step of knowing Jesus personally. I said, "We have to stop here because I am getting attached." We had a talk and went our separate ways for a month or so. - Will

Because she wasn't where she needed to be spiritually, you walked away—even though it broke your heart? You were willing to walk away from the relationship until she took that next step? — Jim

I did. It hurt. It was the worst thing I've ever done. I don't know if Mark or Bob remember that time, but I bawled my eyes out. I was upset and it was hard. I think God honored that and brought her in. He said if you set something free, he'll give it back to you. I think that's what happened. - Will

How long should you wait before you get physically involved? How physically involved should dating couples become? — Jim

Hand holding. – Scotia

Hand holding? Honest? — Jim

That is as far as I'm going. Having been sexually active before I was walking with Christ, I personally wouldn't be satisfied with just kissing. Holding hands is as far as I'm going to go. That is the standard I have set. – Scotia

You're not going to kiss a man, until you kiss him in the aisle? — Jim

That's what I want. This standard has lasted so far. I have kissed guys since I have been walking with Christ. It [messes] up the whole relationship. The focus stops being on learning to communicate through words. It starts being a big intimacy thing, and I feel like it ruins the relationship. – Scotia

What did it take the focus off? — Jim

It took the focus off learning about each other. We felt like we knew each other because we kissed. It made us feel closer than we really were. When you become physically involved with somebody, romance tends to take over. You don't even necessarily have to have sex, but you become disillusioned with the romance, because it's going to be gone at some point. It comes down to a commitment, then the romance comes and goes. It's more important to develop mutual respect first and to learn how that individual thinks and reacts in various situations. – Scotia

No kissing. Let me hear some responses to that. Could you do it? — Jim

No, I don't think so. — Ben

I think it's weird. That would be my first reaction. I can't imagine not even kissing someone. — John

What if you found out that the girl you were dating and were going to marry had never kissed anyone but you? — Jim

It would be weird. — John

But would you like it? Would it be a turn-on or a turnoff? — Jim

I don't know. — John

I can see that being a reasonable expectation. Physically, once one thing happens, it's very easy for things to progress. I need to go into a relationship saying, "I'm not going to spend the night at his house, I'm not going to lie next to him or I'm not going to do this." Maybe the first couple of times, these things would be OK, but if one of you are feeling weak or whatever... once one thing happens, it's easy for it to lead to something else. — Vicki

It has to be a commitment that both of you make. I can't just make that commitment alone. The other person has to also. There will be times when I want to kiss; it's not like I don't want to kiss. It's a choice that I've made. — Scotia

So, you're not denying your sexual attraction? You're saying that there is one, but you can't go there right now? — Jim

Oh no, I'm not pretending to be plastic or anything. — Scotia

I can't imagine not doing that. I'm not saying she's wrong for what she's set as a standard. I don't think anyone really knows exactly how far. It's not like there's a rule book telling you that you should do this or that. I think each individual has to decide on his or her limits. - John

I wish I could be like Scotia; I don't think it's possible. I'm just not as strong as she is. - Ben

What's your line you won't cross? — Jim

The problem is when you start making out. I can see giving someone a kiss good night, but when you're sitting on the couch, kissing for an hour, there's no way. You're going to get messed up; something's going to happen. That would be an area where you are looking for danger. I totally respect what Scotia said, but I can also see a guy giving a girl a good-night kiss. You have to be careful not to push your levels of temptation. - Mark

What if a person that you're dating has had an active sex life? Does that make you just another person? Does that make you feel special? - Will

I never thought about it. The first person that I had sex with was my first boyfriend. None of that crossed my mind. - Vicki

This is a big philosophy that's out there . . . in books or magazines. I've heard people say that you have to experiment with different people to make sure it's right, to test-drive the car to see how it handles. - Will

144

I think it is a bunch of bull for people to say that. I have friends who have said similar things. "What if I get married to this person and the sex isn't good?" My whole philosophy is that if you are so in love with that person, everything you do together is going to be phenomenal, because love is the foundation of the relationship and that will make it awesome. I think for people who say that, it's a way of justifying it or saying it's OK, because they have to see if they like it. - Lisa

I take more of the "I have to see if I like it approach." I dated one Christian guy. He was cool and I was really attracted to him mentally, but physically I couldn't picture myself being involved with him. Maybe I wasn't attracted to him. But the thought did cross my mind, "I don't know if he'd be good." I don't think that I was physically attracted to him at all. - Vicki

You can have great sex with someone. But what about the other 23 hours in a day? You have to be able to look at someone, have a conversation and eat dinner with that person. — Jim

I agree with what Lisa said about love. Being married to someone and having sex with that person for two years, the best sex you have are the moments when you're very intimate-not physically-but spiritually and emotionally. That's where long-lasting sexual pleasure comes from. I don't know if you've ever had that with someone, if you've had different sexual partners. The most important thing is to find someone you love and can communicate with on other levels besides physical. That's the least of the levels of communication. You have an emotional-intellectual level, but ultimately you communicate on a spiritual level. If those things are all right, then I think your sex life is going to fall into place. Vicki, the guy you referred to wasn't meant for you. I don't think God calls you to marry somebody that you are not physically attracted to. - Mark

I won't date someone just for the sake of dating. I don't want to date someone and lead him on for the sake of satisfying my own selfish needs. - Scotia

The real issue out there is the reality that someone might become pregnant as a result of an active sex life, but I never felt used. - Vicki

What went through your mind when you thought that you might be pregnant? — Jim

I was at a party. I just knew. I didn't have to take a pregnancy test. I said, "Dude, I'm pregnant. I know I am." - Vicki

Was it your first boyfriend? — Jim

Yeah, I was 15 years old. My friend was with me when I took a pregnancy test. I told her to look at the results. I closed my eyes. She flipped on the light and looked at me with tears rolling down her cheeks and told me it was positive. I didn't think, "Oh, this is a kid, or anything like that." I called the guy and told him that he better come up with $300, because I was pregnant and then I hung up the phone. I froze and I shut down. It all happened so fast.

I went into Planned Parenthood. I said, "Don't tell me I'm going to kill it, don't tell me it's a kid, don't tell me anything—this is what I'm doing. It's my choice." I put up walls. All that I thought about was how I had to get out of it. It's hard to say how you would help somebody else, because a person in that situation isn't thinking clearly and doesn't have her head on her shoulders like it should be. - Vicki

No, they found out. I had the abortion done on a Friday. This lady called my house and told my mom that she wanted her to know that I had had an abortion, then she hung up the phone. My mom came and picked me up from work and asked me if it had happened. I told her yes, and then I ran away from home. My mom was mad because I told someone else's mom. I didn't feel comfortable telling her. - Vicki

Why couldn't you talk to your mom? - Will

I didn't feel comfortable. - Vicki

Was your mom upset because you had the abortion, or was she more concerned about the fact that you hadn't told her about it? — Jim

In a way, I think she was mad because I told someone else and I didn't tell her. I had already decided that I wasn't going to tell my mom. I didn't feel comfortable at all. But, I did tell my brother about it. He was cool. Now, he comes to me to talk about things like that. The fear of what I experienced is a witness. My friends all know that I went through that and I think it makes them more cautious. What happened to me is a witness, a hard one, but I think that my situation does have an impact on them. Later, I went to church camp. I had moments where I stood up in front of 1,500 people. I felt the Spirit working in my life. Since that time, I've felt OK about it. - Vicki

Jim asked the guys in the group

what they would do if they found out that their girlfriend was pregnant.

John: "If you're not responsible for what is going to happen afterwards, then you're not responsible to do it. If that were to happen to me, I would accept full responsibility."

Jim: "What does that mean? Would you marry her?"

John: "I don't know. Probably not, if I wasn't in love with her. I don't think it would be fair to the kid for us to be married and be miserable throughout its childhood. I would rather the child have two happy parents, who are good friends and have a good relationship—who aren't married. I would rather the child grow up with two happy families, than be in a family where everyone hates each other."

Jim: "Would you want to be involved in your child's life?"

John: "I definitely would want to be involved in my child's life. I don't ever see myself ditching out on a kid. I know people who have done that."

Jim: "Would you consider abortion as an option?"

John: "If it's up to me, no. I would take care of other people's kids, if it would prevent an abortion."

Jim: "It's your child as much as it is the mother's child."

John: "Ultimately, she is going to make the decision whether or not to have the child. I can influence her decision and tell her not to, but she makes the final decision. I can't really tell her no, but I can tell her how I feel. She's the one who is going to have the child."

David: "I feel like John. I wouldn't want the girl to have an abortion. It is killing a baby. The fact that she's pregnant is the result of a mistake, but I don't think you should give the baby up."

Vicki: "I regret the way I put up walls. If I had it to do over again or if I were giving someone advice, it would be different. At the time I had the abortion, I don't feel like it was a choice. I don't think I would have been open to what anyone said because my heart was hardened. Afterwards, I realized that it really was a kid. What people don't talk about is how it affects you mentally. It messes with your head."

At what point in a relationship do you talk about dating standards and how physically involved you will become? — Jim

If you establish a friendship first, you will feel comfortable talking about it. — Scotia

It needs to be said before you become physically involved. — Lisa

Both myself and the girl I'm dating now are strong Christians. We talked about it two or three weeks into the relationship. — David

I really think sexual temptation is the number one issue for a lot of people. Even after you're married, you still deal with certain issues, like lust or temptation. It's a matter of holiness. It's about following the Spirit and not pushing your limits. — Mark

What if you're in a relationship and you are more physically involved than you should be—what should you do? How can you stop? — Jim

I think you have to go "cold turkey" and focus on developing your friendship. That will help you determine where God wants the relationship to go. Once you pass certain boundaries, it's easy to go there again. The best thing to do is not put yourself in a situation where you'll be tested. Don't be alone, go on a double-date. — Mark

We're not strong and if we put ourselves in that situation, we have to be careful. — Lisa

How far are you going to take it, before you give in? You can prevent things from happening. That's important to me. You realize that when you're in a certain environment that you're comfortable in, and others, you're not. You have to keep yourself out of situations that cause temptation. — David

I've never dated anyone, or kissed anyone. I know there are people who can relate to my situation and they wonder if people think that they may become a nun. That's not necessarily God's plan. I really feel like God is preparing me right now for relationships that I will establish in the future. - Rachel

That's awesome. - Mark

How do you deal with the fact that you've gone too far? — Jim

It's done and over with. Some people feel like it's a big issue of repentance, but I have chosen a different way now. I don't necessarily feel regret. - Vicki

I think it's different for every person. . . . I struggle with myself and what I've done. I haven't had sex. I struggle with how to tell my future wife what I have done. I can ask God for forgiveness and I know he's forgiven me, because I've been sincere about it. But, it still eats at my insides. When you ask for forgiveness, you are forgiven and you can go on. Sex and marriage should be special and I think they can be.
- David

Ultimately, it's about God's way. Your whole life is about fulfilling God's plan. It isn't about feeling guilty. God can restore life.
- Mark

After we finished our discussion,

we walked around the mall for about an hour. The majority of us wanted to get our hair either dyed or cut. We really didn't have enough time to have it done at the mall, so we went back to the venue and had a hair-dying/bleaching party in AudioA's dressing room. Red hair was the popular choice, but we think Mark went a little too far. His hair was fire-engine red by the time we were finished.

While that was going on, AudioA was auditioning a guitarist from Minneapolis.

We ate dinner together for the last time. Everyone was gearing up to say good-bye, but no one was looking forward to it. The concert that night was awesome. It was the biggest concert of the whole week, and we got to watch it from the front of the stage. It blew us away when Mark introduced us from the stage and invited us up to perform "Big House" with them—the last song of their set.

After we finished, we took pictures backstage, then headed to the bus, in preparation for the 16-hour bus ride back to Nashville. We ate pizza, prayed for a safe journey for us, and for AudioA— as they were traveling on to Fargo, ND. All good things must come to an end, but we didn't want this experience to end so soon. The week was filled with many intense moments that we will not soon forget. We are all better because of it.

It was our last day with AudioA and the others. What an amazing trip! It was truly a trip of a lifetime. It has completely blown me away. Weeks ago, I would have never imagined going on tour with AudioA. We were able to sing "Big House" on stage in front of 10,000–12,000 people. It was a dream come true. God loves me so much. — Chad

It will be weird to see what happens when we go home.
- Vicki

Today's topic on sex and dating was hard. Kids don't realize how much Christians can fall, especially when they start to compromise on what God calls sex and dating to be. It starts with the hint of compromise, and slowly the compromise becomes bigger. We need to learn to set standards and draw lines. How will you know to stop when it's wrong? Some people get disillusioned that sex is just a part of dating. We need to show that you can date without becoming physically involved.
- Lisa

What does God think

about sex?

"Flee from sexual immorality. All other sins a man commits are outside his body, but he who sins sexually sins against his own body. Do you not know that your body is a temple of the Holy Spirit, who is in you, whom you have received from God? You are not your own; you were bought at a price. Therefore honor God with your body."
1 Corinthians 6:18-20 NIV "Put to death, therefore, whatever belongs to your earthly nature: sexual immorality, impurity, lust, evil desires and greed, which is idolatry."
Colossians 3:5 NIV "Can you build a fire in your lap and not burn your pants? Can you walk barefoot on hot coals and not get blisters? It's the same when you have sex with your neighbor's man's wife: Touch her and you'll pay for it. No excuses." Proverbs 6:27-29 THE MESSAGE

More than half of all teens have sex by age 18. Even in our churches, 27% of youth have had intercourse by age 18 and 20% believe that sex outside of marriage is morally acceptable. Sexually transmitted diseases infect 3,000,000 teenagers annually.

"I really feel like God is preparing me right **now for relationships** that I will establish in the future." — Rachel

"We've really grown attached to all these people. I know our prayers will be with them as we go our separate ways." — Mark

After Words

Will

I think our discussions will provide a cutting-edge tool for youth ministers. When I was in youth group, there were a lot of areas we would never talk about. Some of those issues were brought up this week. I think that kids generally don't open up to people. Maybe if they see others sharing, it might help them open up more. This book can be used as a tool to help them talk about a subject and it can have a positive effect on their youth group.

I liked Vicki a lot because she reminds me of my twin sister. They both are spunky, very outgoing and willing to say what they think—without holding back anything. I'm very positive, so I'll usually water it down, or maybe color it a little bit so that it feels a little better. I like Vicki's boldness.

The thing that got me excited about this project is that it is a progressive approach to youth ministry. It's something that hasn't been done before. We have the opportunity to use media and music to stir things up within the youth group. Youth are being exposed to a lot of cool things in the media. Why shouldn't the church get involved with all the media available to combat what their teenagers are being bombarded with? This project is something that's cool and fresh that people can relate to.

Ben

Taking the road trip with these guys is something that we've never done before. I've been with the band for over a year and a half, and it's the first time we've done this. I really like to think that we could say that we do this kind of thing all the time and we love to reach out to people.

At first, I wondered about why we were doing it now. But, meeting all the people on the trip has really opened my eyes—it kind of throws a brick at your head. I grew up in suburbia with rich kids, and we thought that people like this existed only in strange places. I think in the last seven days I have seen a total change in some of the people on the trip. I can think of a certain girl; I won't mention any names. She hasn't cussed as much toward the end of the week; not to say that if you cuss that you're going to Hell, but she's just been around people who don't cuss.

I used to cuss a lot and when I was around people who didn't cuss, it changed my perspective. Then when I heard someone who did cuss, I thought that they sounded like a sailor and it sounded stupid to me. This trip has been a real eye-opener.

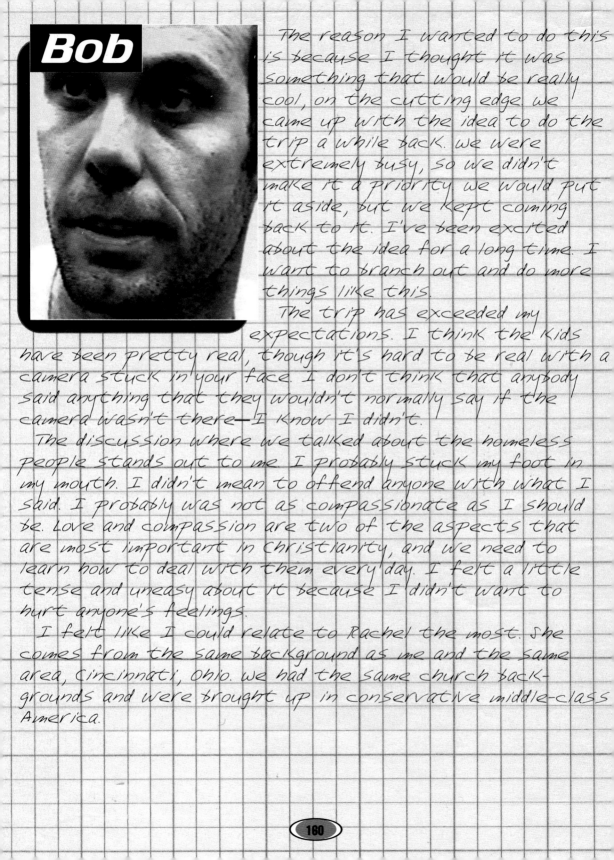

Bob

The reason I wanted to do this is because I thought it was something that would be really cool, on the cutting edge. We came up with the idea to do the trip a while back. We were extremely busy, so we didn't make it a priority. We would put it aside, but we kept coming back to it. I've been excited about the idea for a long time. I want to branch out and do more things like this.

The trip has exceeded my expectations. I think the kids have been pretty real, though it's hard to be real with a camera stuck in your face. I don't think that anybody said anything that they wouldn't normally say if the camera wasn't there—I know I didn't.

The discussion where we talked about the homeless people stands out to me. I probably stuck my foot in my mouth. I didn't mean to offend anyone with what I said. I probably was not as compassionate as I should be. Love and compassion are two of the aspects that are most important in Christianity, and we need to learn how to deal with them every day. I felt a little tense and uneasy about it because I didn't want to hurt anyone's feelings.

I felt like I could relate to Rachel the most. She comes from the same background as me and the same area, Cincinnati, Ohio. We had the same church backgrounds and were brought up in conservative middle-class America.

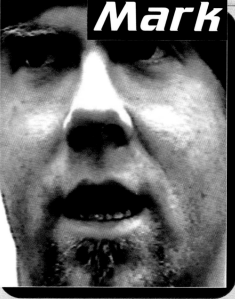

Mark

We thought it would really be cool to pick kids from around the country, with various backgrounds and different levels of commitment to Jesus Christ—and put them on the road with Audio Adrenaline. We wanted it to be used as a youth group tool. God really opened a lot of different doors and started blessing all the different ideas that we had and everybody came together on the same page.

The experience has definitely exceeded my expectations. We've seen the expressions of the kids and that's been really powerful for me. Some of the topics were really heated and others were really shocking. I think God was really involved with the planning of this whole thing. I'm really happy with what's happened here.

The discussion about the family stands out to me the most. It was really powerful. It gave me the opportunity to see someone else's perspective. I came from a normal, real conservative, Christian family with a mom and dad. To see the other side of the tracks was really shocking for me—hearing Vicki talk about what it's like to not even have a relationship with her father, hearing Scotia talk about how it took her three years to start talking to her dad. I know Rachel was moved by that whole topic, as well. There are a lot of kids out there who are dealing with a great deal of pain and it will really hit home for them.

As far as relating to the people on the trip, there's definitely a place in my heart for Chad. I don't want to sound like I'm having any pity on him, but I look at him and don't even think about his leg as a deterrent. He has such a positive attitude. He's just so encouraging and I'm in awe of what he has done. He's a powerful young man in the midst of the circumstances that he faces. I don't want to single anyone out, they're all beautiful people. It's been a great trip. We hope that they will always remain in God.

I also want to say thanks to the kids for being so vulnerable. They were selfless; this has been a lot of work. It challenged us and was painful at times. I think a lot of others will be able to grow closer to God. God bless you guys—hopefully we'll do it again.

David

One of the neatest things that happened on the trip was just being up front and on stage with Audio Adrenaline, when they were filming the concert. It was great to see the concert from that close, because the first night we were way in the back. It was also good to see how it feels to be on the road. We saw how tiring it is, and all those feelings that go with it. We saw how they worked together and what life on the road is really like.

One of the lessons that stood out to me the most was learning to not generalize or criticize people, but to look at who they really are on the inside. I think we need to go beyond their outside appearance and what they look like. It doesn't matter what clothes they are wearing or how many times their ears are pierced. You have to forget about all that and really have to see who a person is—it's then that you should decide if you like the person or not. I'm going to work on that when I get home.

The most difficult part was learning to get along with everyone. I felt like I always had to be in a great mood, which was hard for me. Sometimes I get tired easily and I don't feel like talking. The discussions were pretty difficult too, because they weren't like just sitting down for 30 minutes to talk about something. They were long and emotional, so that was a tough part.

I hope that people who read the book realize how neat the experience was for us. Most of us came into this thinking that it was going to be so cool, rather than what we were going to accomplish through the discussions. Now that we've done it, I really do hope that others get something out of it. When they see all of the various personality types that we represent, I think that everyone can identify with one of us in some way. I hope the advice that we've given and the solutions that we came up with can be applied to other people's lives.

One of the trip's highlights was bonding with a great group of people. We all had different perspectives. I learned to appreciate everybody for who he or she is. We had to find a middle ground of connection—I really enjoyed that. As I look back on this time, I am going to remember the people. With the seven of us and the band, I think everyone was really awesome.

One thing that moved me was that we were faced with dealing with reality. It challenged me to look inside myself and really express how I felt. It wasn't just about the "Christian thing," or what a Christian should say, even though I believe that. It made me take a deeper look at what I believe and why. God calls us to live out our faith.

One of the most challenging aspects was dealing with someone who couldn't grasp the reality and fullness of who God is. During the talks, we would have to sit and listen to other people's beliefs and opinions. We had to be able to respect what they were each saying. I believe 110 percent that God is a reality. It's a frustrating thing to deal with someone who can't understand that. You have to sit back and know they can have it, even though they don't have it, or they don't want it.

I hope that when other people learn about our trip and experiences they can connect in some way to something that we did or said. I hope they can relate to us and realize that whatever experiences they face, they still have God to rely on. I hope it gives them the motivation to have a personal relationship with God and depend on him no matter what happens.

Chad

Just hanging out with Audio Adrenaline was the highlight of my week. I've liked them and their music for years. I think people have a tendency to elevate artists and performers in their minds. The first two days I could hardly believe that I was on the road with them. This week I've seen that they're just normal people. I learned a lot about their personal lives and what they believe. They are all really nice guys.

The toughest thing about the trip was dealing with the topics in such depth. The first night at Ben's house was a pretty personal and indepth look at our lives. I was really moved when Scotia and Vicki told about what they've gone through.

I wasn't expecting to get so deeply involved in the topics, but I'm glad we did. The one that hit me the most was probably when we talked about our prejudices. Scotia shared that she was offended. I didn't say anything directly, but I kind of felt responsible for that. I tend to feel uncomfortable when other people feel uncomfortable.

I hope that people will be able to relate to us and the experiences that we've shared (especially new Christians). If someone sees me and says, "Hey, I have a disability too," maybe what I've shared will help. I think it was the intention of us all to ultimately bring glory to God. It's a God-driven thing and I hope people will see that. I hope that younger teenagers will realize how much God loves them and wants to influence their lives.

The most valuable part of this trip is the relationships I've made. When we started on the trip, I didn't know anyone. Now, I know six other people who are my age that live all across the country. I also know the band, which is weird.

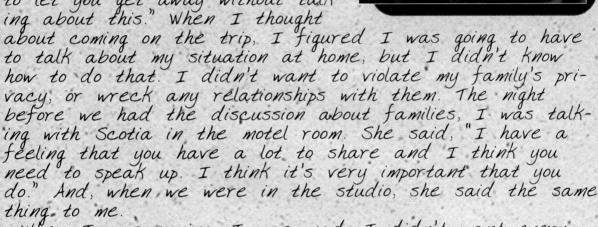

One of the memorable topics for me was at Horizons Studio, when I was crying in front of the camera. I just wanted to be by myself, but I couldn't because there was a camera in my face. I felt God saying, "I'm not going to let you get away without talk- ing about this." When I thought about coming on the trip, I figured I was going to have to talk about my situation at home, but I didn't know how to do that. I didn't want to violate my family's pri- vacy, or wreck any relationships with them. The night before we had the discussion about families, I was talk- ing with Scotia in the motel room. She said, "I have a feeling that you have a lot to share and I think you need to speak up. I think it's very important that you do." And, when we were in the studio, she said the same thing to me.

When I was crying, I was mad. I didn't want every- body to be there. I just wanted to wallow in it by myself. God wasn't letting me; he was saying, "No, this is your opportunity to share—there are people who need to hear your testimony and I'm not going to let you get away with this. You have to talk about it and trust me to work out all the details."

I hope people can identify with one of us, or many of us, somehow. We asked a lot of questions and we have seen how God can work through various situations. I'm not this great model Christian; I'm not perfect, but I hope people can identify with that.

Vicki

The best part of the trip for me was the individual conversations that I had with people—certain people in the group. I remember the heartfelt conversations I had with John, Scotia, Ginny and Dale. I enjoyed the one-on-one conversations more than those with the group as a whole. It gave me an opportunity to get to know each person.

The topic that moved me the most was probably the day when I started crying. Once you cry, you break, but you feel better. Everyone had seen me cry and I didn't have any more walls to put up. My cards were already laid on the table and there was really nothing left for me to hide. It was hard, but it was good for me personally.

I didn't like the fact that we were constantly on the go. I wish I had more time to be by myself. I don't feel like I belong in a group. I feel like I have to fight for attention and I don't want to deal with it. Overall, I feel God was involved with what was going on. When other people learn about what we've done, I hope they can see how real the experience was and how serious the topics are.

When I reflect back on the trip, I'll remember the one-on-one conversations that I had. In the motel room with Rachel, we really had the opportunity to sit down and talk. I also learned how to golf and I really liked it. I always thought it was boring when I would watch it on television, but when I did it, I enjoyed it.

Scotia

In the first discussion, "Do You Know How I Feel?" Vicki was talking about putting up walls. I was sitting there telling her that she put up walls, but I realized that I put them up too. I saw firsthand how past relationships and experiences have caused me to establish a defense mechanism to shut everybody out. Now I understand why I behave the way I do, and why other people respond the way that they do. That's probably been the most life-changing thing that I've learned.

The most challenging time was when we came back from talking with the homeless. Some comments were made that I felt were very insensitive. We were standing in the subway talking, but I really felt like I was alone. It was snowing and I went outside in the freezing cold-I remember crying because I felt like the black people who saw me walk by with this group of white people rejected me. One guy purposely bumped me, then I heard the comments that were made within the group and I felt rejection on all sides. That to me was a low point I just wanted to go home.

Being involved on the trip gave me the opportunity to offer my perspective about the things that were being discussed. I don't think we resolved every issue, in every conversation; that comes through having relationships with other people and understanding who they are as people. When I first came to know Christ, I had an attitude of doing things 100 percent, but still felt that I'd have to do things alone. I hope others realize that they are not alone. I hope they can see themselves in us.

to go and everyone banded together and went with me. I liked that
a lot.

I think we were all different
when we came here, not really
having anyone to identify with. We
were out of our comfort zones and
we were put in an environment
where we had to deal with the
various personalities involved, as
well as the issues. The topic that I
enjoyed the most was the discussion on piercing. I felt like
I knew more about that topic than any other one.

I hope that others will see seven people who were real
and were able to be themselves. I hope that they can
realize there is someone whom they can relate to.

Minneapolis MN
Saturday March 15, 1997

Aftershow signing
Northwest Bookstore

Meet & Greet
Mark
Be in Dressing Room by 6:45p

Bible Study
1:00p

Show Time
Carolyn 7:30p
Audio Adrenaline 7:50p

Tomorrow
Fargo ND
239 Miles, 3.75 hrs
Same Time Zone

What They're Doing Now

Just before we went to press, we decided to call the seven souls and ask a few more questions. Here's what we asked and what they said:

Reflecting on the trip, is there anything you would do or say differently?

I would definitely talk a lot more, and not be so concerned about what other people thought about what I was saying - Rachel

I would have spoken my mind a little bit more concerning how individuals were acting. - John

Overall, I'd probably be more bold. - David

MAYBE I WOULD HAVE BEEN A LITTLE MORE OUTGOING. IT WAS A NEW SITUATION AND I NOTICED I WAS KEEPING TO MYSELF MORE THAN USUAL. I WOULD HAVE WISHED THE BAND, CREW AND EVERYONE WOULD KEEP IN TOUCH. — CHAD

I wish I would have been more vulnerable. Sometimes because of the group size or time limitations, I don't feel like the discussions reached a deep level of honesty. I wish I would have been real and right up front instead of waiting. - Lisa

I wish I had made more of an effort to get to know Lisa better. The last night I got a glimpse of the "real Lisa"—the sensitive side that doesn't have it all together. I would have pursued that earlier in the week. - Scotia

I would have acted differently in some conversations. Sometimes there should have been more controversy. For example, I thought the discussion on marriage and the family was stupid. No one knows exactly what they'll be doing—I don't think it will help someone out when they grow up. - Vicki

Overall, what did you think of the experience?

I feel overwhelmed. I think I was really blessed to be a part of it. I'm very thankful for the experience and how God chose everyone who went. We had a diverse group of people and God worked through us all individually. I think the whole thing was a maturity process. I liked touring on the bus, but it was pretty cramped. - Rachel

I'm glad I went on the trip, but I don't think that I walked away with any new knowledge. It was a great time. - John

Man, it was awesome! If I could do it every weekend, I would. - David

IT WAS GREAT. I CAN TRULY SAY IT'S THE BEST THING THAT I'VE EVER DONE. IT WAS SUCH A SPECIAL WEEK. IT'S A BLESSING TO SEE WHERE GOD CAN TAKE YOU WHERE HE WANTS YOU TO BE. HE LOVES US SO MUCH AND WANTS TO DO INCREDIBLE THINGS IN OUR LIVES. HE WANTS TO DO NEW AND BIGGER MIRACLES WITHIN US. — CHAD

I had an awesome time with a great group of people. I'd love to do it again. We had the opportunity to develop intimate friendships. I value the experience and think it was very rewarding. I learned a lot. - Lisa

It was absolutely life-changing. I got a chance to get out of my role as leader of my campus, and as a leader in my church among my peers. It's OK to be flawed and relax and be who I am. I carried that back with me. As a result, I have been able to be more vulnerable, open and authentic. I have been able to break through some walls in my relationships with friends and family. - Scotia

I have a total respect for the people (AudioA and crew), because it's a tough job— it's not all fun and games. - Vicki

What are you doing now?

I am going to school at Anderson University in Anderson, Indiana. I'm think-ing about going into music, business or becoming a teacher. Since the trip, I've also been thinking about mission work and how serious it is. I am try-ing to figure out how I can incorporate it into my life. - Rachel

I'm still working at Metropolis. I'm getting ready to go to school at Saddleback University (in California). I haven't picked a major yet, but I still have a strong interest in filmmaking and producing. I've also been doing video projects with my friends. We're going to start a cable access TV show. We hope to have special guests on the show and include music videos. - John

I just broke my ankle playing football and I had to have surgery on it. I'm really upset because I'll miss most of the football season. Hopefully, I'll be back for the playoff games. We just started school. I'm involved in choir, and I'm the student council presi-dent. I'm disappointed about breaking my ankle. I had my whole senior year planned out, now I'm having to make adjustments. For example, I'm in this musical/drama and we're having to rewrite the script, because there's a lot of dance moves in it. - David

I'M GOING TO SCHOOL AT THE UNIVERSITY OF NORTHERN COLORADO. — CHAD

I'm still going to school, pursuing my psychology degree. I plan on get-ting my masters degree, as well. I'm actively involved in a group called "Discovering Life's Purpose." We work with college students and help them develop their talents and skills, so that they can determine their pur-pose in life. I really have the opportunity to act as a motivator and encourager. I've also started my own cleaning company with a girlfriend. It's called, "Castles and Cottages." - Lisa

This summer I worked for almost three months at a sports camp in Missouri. I spent time with inner-city high-school students. It's amazing to see those kids come from all over the country and get to do all kinds of things they don't normally get to do. I will graduate from Bowie State this December with a B.A. in psychology. I'm also teaching dance with a Christian dance company and tutoring Spanish. - Scotia

I'm going to school at Diablo Valley College, studying general education. Since I got back from the trip, I feel a lot of peace with my family situation. Now I realize how important family really is. Before the trip, I didn't see that as much. - Vicki

R 03:01.29.18

What's the number one thing you walked away from the trip with?

I had a somber realization of how God really works in our lives and how powerful that is. I've really been looking at what I've learned and examining why I believe the way I do. - Rachel

I don't know. It was fun meeting Ben—I liked him a lot. - John

I walked away with a broader world perspective. Being with different people really opened me up to more than just Highland Park. - David

IT WAS GREAT TO GO UP ON STAGE WITH AUDIO ADRENALINE AND JUST HANG OUT WITH THEM. IT WAS ALSO COOL TO CREATE RELATIONSHIPS, AND THE ONES I MADE WITH DAVID AND RACHEL ARE ESPECIALLY MEANINGFUL. — CHAD

I walked away feeling that it was OK to be real. I have a broader appreciation for different people. We have to be willing to love and accept different people for who they are. - Lisa

Life's too short not to be real. I hope kids can see themselves in us. I hope this will teach people that it's OK to be very different from everyone around you and still be a Christian—as long as those differences aren't sin. Christians deal with real issues and have real struggles and that's OK. - Scotia

It was just cool. I really like Scotia a lot. - Vicki

Jim

Jim Burgen *was the road pastor for the trip. His job was to facilitate the discussion of the seven issues. Here are some of his reflections on the trip:*

The locker-room scene at Market Square Arena redefined the whole week. I felt like it got beyond surface issues and got to the heart. The seven individuals called me out and I called them out. One of the toughest parts of the trip was often having to play the devil's advocate in order to get people to talk. Sometimes I would have to represent something I wouldn't normally say—the body piercing discussion comes to mind.

My whole heart is to create an environment that allows a student to check out this "God thing." The trip reminded me that everybody comes with his baggage—his or her own background and life story. Those that came on the trip ran the spectrum from Ozzie and Harriet to some highly dysfunctional families. And, yet, they were all looking for the same thing. Everyone desperately wanted to believe in and follow God. They wanted to express truth, but sometimes didn't know how to put it in words, or they didn't share out of fear. They all wanted to know what God thinks about these issues, and how they are supposed to live out their faith in daily life. I think a lot of other people want to know the same things.

01:32:20.22
PLAY   LOCK

CD-ROM INFORMATION

Hidden on this AudioVision CD are artist interviews, full-length videos and much more. To try the disc, you'll need at least an MPC II Windows or Mac 040 computer with 5 MB available RAM and a 2x CD-ROM drive. Because Enhanced CD technology is brand new, these minimum configurations can't guarantee that the disc will perform on every system, but most computers will play the disc, and we hope yours is one of them. If you encounter any difficulties, please visit this website for help: http://www.ardentrecords.com/

On a Windows Machine
1) Ensure Windows is running.
2) Access the file manager.
3) Double-click the ZOMBIE CDROM drive.
4) Double-click on README.txt.

On a Macintosh
1) Double-click the CDROM icon on your desktop.
2) Double-click on README (MAC).
Some CD-ROM drives will read these discs as audio only and you will not be able to access the data. If this happens, contact your computer manufacturer and let them know you want to support Enhanced CDs. Anyway, we hope you enjoy the music.

A small percentage of CD audio players not manufactured to proper specifications may attempt to play the computer data as music. This could be both unpleasant and potentially damaging to your stereo system if you don't take the following precautions the first time you play your AVCD:
1) Turn the volume all the way down on your stereo system.
2) Press "play" on your CD player.
3) Slowly bring up the volume. If you hear any static-like noise, use the skip forward controls on your CD player to advance to the next track.

(If you don't encounter any noise or other problems during the above procedure, it will not be necessary to repeat the process on subsequent plays.) Due to the high demands of interactive multimedia CD-ROM software and the large number of different computer configurations, the smooth operation of each particular configuration cannot be guaranteed.